At Issue

Adaptation and
Climate Change

Other Books in the At Issue Series:

At Issue

Adaptation and Climate Change

Sarah Flint Erdreich, Book Editor

GREENHAVEN PRESS
A part of Gale, Cengage Learning

GALE
CENGAGE Learning

Detroit • New York • San Francisco • New Haven, Conn • Waterville, Maine • London

Christine Nasso, *Publisher*
Elizabeth Des Chenes, *Managing Editor*

© 2009 Greenhaven Press, a part of Gale, Cengage Learning.

Gale and Greenhaven Press are registered trademarks used herein under license.

For more information, contact:
Greenhaven Press
27500 Drake Rd.
Farmington Hills, MI 48331-3535
Or you can visit our Internet site at gale.cengage.com

For product information and technology assistance, contact us at

Gale Customer Support, 1-800-877-4253
For permission to use material from this text or product, submit all requests online at www.cengage.com/permissions

Further permissions questions can be emailed to permissionrequest@cengage.com

Articles in Greenhaven Press anthologies are often edited for length to meet page requirements. In addition, original titles of these works are changed to clearly present the main thesis and to explicitly indicate the author's opinion. Every effort is made to ensure that Greenhaven Press accurately reflects the original intent of the authors. Every effort has been made to trace the owners of copyrighted material.

Cover photograph © Debra Hughes 2007. Used under license from Shutterstock.com.

LIBRARY OF CONGRESS CATALOGING-IN-PUBLICATION DATA

Adaptation and climate change / Sarah Flint Erdreich, book editor.
    p. cm. -- (At issue)
    Includes bibliographical references and index.
    ISBN 978-0-7377-4276-3 (hardcover)
    ISBN 978-0-7377-4275-6 (pbk.)
    1. Human beings--Effect of climate on. 2. Adaptation (Biology) 3. Global environmental change. 4. Climatic changes--Environmental aspects. I. Erdreich, Sarah Flint.
    GF71.A37 2009
    304.2'5--dc22

                                                                2008053996

Printed in the United States of America
1 2 3 4 5 6 7 13 12 11 10 09

Contents

Introduction

In October 2007, the Nobel Prize committee announced that the year's recipients of the Nobel Peace Prize were former U.S. Vice President Al Gore and the Intergovernmental Panel on Climate Change. Gore and the IPCC received the award in part for "their efforts to build up and disseminate greater knowledge about man-made climate change, and to lay the foundations for the measures that are needed to counteract such change."

By awarding the Peace Prize to a controversial issue that had been framed primarily in terms of science and environmental issues in the past, the Nobel committee cast the climate change debate in a larger context, one in which Gore and other activists had long been arguing that climate change belonged. The justification for considering climate change a peace issue was, in large part, the belief that environmental problems affect human security, which in turn affects peace both within individual nations and between nations. In his presentation speech, the chairman of the Norwegian Nobel Committee, Professor Ole Danbolt Mjøs, cited conflicts in Darfur and other regions in Africa where changing climate patterns mean that individuals from different tribes clash over access to the diminishing number of fertile areas in regions throughout the continent. Professor Mjøs also noted that the diminishing ice in the Arctic is making the question of which nations can lay claim to the area more urgent. That issue is examined in more detail later in this anthology.

With this award, the Nobel committee ushered a growing scientific concern to the forefront of the world's consciousness. For decades, members of the scientific community had warned that the temperature of the earth was increasing, and that this could have dire effects for both humans and animals, as well as the earth itself. Sharing their concerns were a number of politicians and private citizens. But for just as long, other scientists, politicians, and citizens have argued that it is difficult to establish conclusively that the earth is growing warmer and that even if the temperature were increasing, it would not necessarily be a harbinger of disaster and upheaval.

While a consensus may never truly be reached, the issue of climate change has already affected the ways that people look at the earth, particularly in terms of how individual lifestyles can impact the environment. Since the beginning of the 21st century, mainstream car companies have introduced hybrid vehicles, local governments have banned the use of plastic bags, and the idea of buying environmentally sustainable products has become increasingly popular. And these are only a few ways in which consumers are altering their purchasing behaviors.

Changes are also occurring on a larger scale. Politicians worldwide debate how best to cut down on the emission of greenhouse gases, which are considered to be the principal contributors to climate change. An equally contentious topic is how, if at all, to regulate greenhouse gas emissions in developing countries, which until relatively recently lagged far behind industrialized nations in terms of greenhouse gas output.

What will the result of all the changes be? Right now, it's still too early to tell. Policies could take months, if not years, to be made into law, and while certain consumer trends seem headed in the direction of adapting to a warmer world, those trends have yet to be adopted by the majority of Americans. But the statement made by the Nobel Peace Prize committee signaled that a tipping point has been reached. Americans are realizing that climate change is a valid concern, and even though adaptation may not happen voluntarily or on as large a scale as some scientists believe it must occur, interest in, and awareness of, adaptation and protection of the earth are at the highest levels they have been in decades.

International concern about climate change, combined with rising oil prices in the spring and summer of 2008 and heightened citizen interest about individual impact on the planet, has raised many questions about how best to adapt behaviors and lifestyles. In *At Issue: Adaptation and Climate Change*, the authors debate how great the threat of climate change is, and explore the myriad ways individuals can shape their relationships with the earth.

1

Climate Change Could Be Devastating and People Must Adapt to Survive

Margareta Wahlström

Margareta Wahlström is the former assistant secretary-general for humanitarian affairs of the United Nations.

Incidents of natural hazards—including floods, droughts, and hurricanes—have increased over the past three decades, and many scientists link this increase to climate change. The aftermath of these disasters often leads to an increased risk to human health in the form of contaminated water and malnutrition, diminished food and water supplies, threats to peace that result when resources are scarce and therefore fought over, and increased migration as people must leave their communities to search for new homes. All of these elements mean that climate change must be considered a threat to human rights as well as an environmental danger. With education, careful planning, and government aid, communities can adapt to climate change and reduce their risk of harm from natural disasters, but such changes can only come about with a firm commitment to mobilize people and invest in life-saving measures.

Climate change is an issue so large in scope and so potentially overwhelming in importance that it might be helpful for us to pause and focus our attention on practical steps we can take to adapt to a warming planet and reduce its negative impacts.

Margareta Wahlström, "Before the Next Disaster Strikes: The Humanitarian Impact of Climate Change," *UN Chronicle*, June 2007. Reprinted with the permission of the United Nations. http://www.un.org.

Consider the adaptation mechanisms of two mammals: polar bears and humans. Polar bears have evolved over thousands of years to adapt to a harsh climate. But today we see these magnificent animals stranded on melting ice floes, struggling to stay afloat. They have no time to adapt and could be extinct in a few decades. And what about humans? How will we stay afloat with rising sea levels, more extreme weather, intensive storms, flooding, heatwaves and droughts coming our way, as scientists agree they will? Unlike polar bears, we can adapt more readily to protect ourselves from natural disasters, including the many effects of global warming. Using simple, cost-effective methods, we can save lives, lands and livelihoods. We have the knowledge and experience to make a critical difference in reducing risks. What is needed is the will to do so now before the next disaster strikes.

Our Increased Vulnerability to Disaster

Indeed, we have no time to waste. Over the past 30 years, disasters—storms, floods and droughts—have increased threefold, according to the UN [United Nations] International Strategy for Disaster Reduction (ISDR). In 2006 alone, 134 million people suffered from natural hazards that cost $35 billion in damages, including the devastating droughts in China and Africa, in addition to massive flooding throughout Asia and Africa. These disasters scarred lives, shattered families, stripped away livelihoods and set back development efforts.

Not only are natural hazards becoming more frequent, but rapid urbanization and population growth mean more people are now at risk. Disasters triggered by these hazards have affected five times more people than they did only a generation ago. Megacities like Tokyo, built on seismic areas, or exposed coastlines like Shanghai, are at particular risk. In such cities as Mumbai, Cairo, Mexico City and Lagos, each with more than 10 million residents, decaying infrastructure, land erosion, crowded conditions and a paucity of rescue services could spell potential calamity should an earthquake or powerful storm hit.

Global warming will exacerbate our growing vulnerability to disasters. As outlined in the Intergovernmental Panel on Climate Change report, hundreds of millions of people will be at increased danger from climate-related hazards. The countries least responsible for global warming—the poorest developing nations—will be the most affected by its consequences, both in human and economic terms. Massive flooding, droughts and storms, the spread of infectious diseases, disruption of crop cycles and competition for natural resources could threaten the lives of millions. Some 200 million people living in coastal flood zones—60 million in South Asia alone—are at risk from intense storms and rising waters. In the cruel calculus of disasters, the poorer the community, the greater its vulnerability to natural hazards and the more difficult its recovery.

The Risks of Climate Change

Given these potential scenarios, the humanitarian community is taking a hard look at how it can help reduce risks, bolster preparedness and respond more effectively to the consequences of climate change. Potential humanitarian impacts include:

Human health risks. Diseases, such as cholera, malaria and dengue fever, will likely increase in some areas as a result of changing temperatures; diarrhoea-related diseases and malnutrition could also climb.

Diminished food security and water supply. Desertification and drought could threaten the livelihoods of over 1 billion people in more than 110 countries, particularly in semi-arid regions.

Rising sea levels. Coastal cities and countries with low coastal areas could be in danger; the Bahamas, Viet Nam, Egypt and Bangladesh are among those at high risk.

Threats to peace and security. Scarcity of key resources, including water, could exacerbate tensions between ethnic groups, countries and regions as they compete for, and adjust to, different environments and resources. Darfur and Sri Lanka are two examples of this potential scenario.

Increased migration and displacement. Populations affected by rising seas, flooding, drought or desertification leave their lands at risk, either voluntarily or by coercion. Some analysts predict we could see up to 50 million environmental refugees by the end of the decade. Environment-related migration has been most acute in sub-Saharan Africa, but also affects millions of people in Asia and India.

Natural disasters need not result in human catastrophe.

How We Can Prepare

What can we do? To begin, we must not be frozen by fear or lulled into a despairing sense of complacency. The greatest risk we face is doing nothing. It is time to roll up our sleeves and get to work in building more disaster-resilient communities. The tools needed are not expensive, particularly given the potential costs. Experts estimate that one dollar invested in risk reduction today can save up to $7 in relief and recovery costs tomorrow. Many of the most effective tools at our disposal to save lives are based on mobilizing people, not on expensive technology. Community-based early warning systems, local disaster education and evacuation plans, better crop and land management techniques are all being completed with great success by nations across the resource spectrum.

Consider Bangladesh, for example, where devastating cyclones swept the country in 1970 and also in 1991, killing half a million people. A community-based "human early warning system" was set up along the Bay of Bengal, and villagers were trained in how to build cyclone shelters, design evacuation plans and other simple measures. The death toll from monsoons and heavy rains in recent years has fallen dramatically. Or take the case of Simeulue Island in Indonesia, situated near the epicentre of the [2004] tsunami. For generations, residents had been taught what to do if an earthquake struck or the ocean suddenly receded, as it did on 26 December 2004: head for the hills. As a result, fewer than ten of the island's 78,000 inhabitants were killed by the giant waves. In nearby Aceh, no such warning system existed; in some areas, up to 90 per cent of the population perished.

The citizens of Toronto, Canada, will benefit from another kind of early warning system, one designed to reduce heat-related deaths. The city has installed an emergency mechanism that will alert public health officials 60 hours before the start of potentially lethal heatwaves, which are expected to increase as the world warms.

For effective disaster preparedness and education, look to Cuba's success. In September 2004, the fifth largest hurricane ever to hit the Caribbean struck the island with winds of 124 miles per hour. Nearly 2 million people—more than 15 per cent of the total population—were safely evacuated and no one was killed. The following summer, Hurricane Dennis hit 12 of Cuba's 14 provinces, affecting some 8 million people, 70 per cent of the population, but thanks to effective community mobilization and evacuation efforts, fewer than 20 died.

Better land use policies, particularly in overpopulated or heavily eroded areas, can also save lives. In 2004, a hurricane killed nearly 3,000 people in Haiti, but caused only a handful of deaths on the other half of the island. The difference: the mangrove trees planted along the Dominican Republic's shoreline buffered high wind and waves, while well-forested hillsides prevented deadly mud slides. Meanwhile, in New Zealand, engineers are pairing up with local governments to strengthen city drainage systems to withstand more intensive rainstorms.

Risk reduction is one of the best insurance policies we can take to protect investment in development. A major disaster can destroy decades of development gains. In Pakistan, the 2005 earthquake cost $5 billion in damages, approximately the same amount the World Bank lent the country over the last decade. In 1998, Hurricane Mitch resulted in losses equal to 41 per cent of Honduras's gross domestic product, while in the Maldives 66 per cent of its GDP [gross domestic product] was wiped out by the 2004 tsunami.

The message is clear: natural disasters need not result in human catastrophe. We must redouble our efforts and invest in simple life-saving measures that can reduce our vulnerability to disasters due to a changing climate. The Global Platform in June 2007, spearheaded by ISDR, will bring together national governments, scientists, non-governmental organizations, financial institutions and the United Nations to move this agenda forward.

The Importance of Education

But disaster-risk reduction is too important to be left to the experts. Risk reduction begins at home, in schools, places of work and worship, and throughout our local communities. It is here where we will either save lives or lose them, depending on the steps we take today to reduce our vulnerability to tomorrow's hazards. For greatest impact, these steps must be grounded in local knowledge and communicated broadly so that everyone, from a local school child to a village grandmother to the municipal mayor, knows how to be protected from nature's vicissitudes.

Education is vital, as is the sharing of experience within and among communities. As importantly, disaster-risk managers need to listen and learn from the grassroots in order to build upon examples of risk reduction that have been tried and tested in the crucible of local experience.

The polar bears are stranded. Let's not leave ourselves open to a similar fate.

2

The Negative Impact of Climate Change Is Overstated

Olaf Stampf (Translated from German by Christopher Sultan)

Olaf Stampf is the head of science and technology for the German news source Spiegel.

A warm Earth does not necessarily portend disaster. As early as 1896, Swedish physicist Svante Arrhenius predicted that rising temperatures would be good for humanity. Arrhenius later won a Nobel Prize; and today, even as world leaders decry climate change, scores of scientists are in agreement with Arrhenius's idea that an increased amount of carbon dioxide in the air can mean better climates and less human suffering. While it is possible that some areas will struggle due to higher temperatures, a number of areas around the world could benefit from stronger harvests, more tourists, and better health. While current climate models make long-term predictions difficult, and the potential negative aspects of rising temperatures should not be discounted, there is still time for people around the world to prepare for climate change in such a way that it does not ruin their communities or livelihoods.

Svante Arrhenius, the father of the greenhouse effect, would be called a heretic today. Far from issuing the sort of dire predictions about climate change which are common nowa-

Olaf Stampf, "Not the End of the World as We Know It," Spiegel Online, May 5, 2007. Reproduced by permission. http://www.spiegel.de.

days, the Swedish physicist dared to predict a paradise on earth for humans when he announced, in April 1896, that temperatures were rising—and that it would be a blessing for all.

Arrhenius, who later won the Nobel Prize in Chemistry, calculated that the release of carbon dioxide—or carbonic acid as it was then known—through burning coal, oil and natural gas would lead to a significant rise in temperatures worldwide. But, he argued, "by the influence of the increasing percentage of carbonic acid in the atmosphere, we may hope to enjoy ages with more equable and better climates," potentially making poor harvests and famine a thing of the past.

Humanity has been reshaping the planet for a very long time, first by clearing forests and plowing fields, and later by building roads, cities and factories.

Arrhenius was merely expressing a view that was firmly entrenched in the collective consciousness of the day: warm times are good times; cold times are bad.

Temperature Patterns in the Past

During the so-called Medieval Warm Period between about 900 and 1300 A.D., for example, the Vikings raised livestock on Greenland and sailed to North America. New cities were built all across Europe, and the continent's population grew from 30 million to 80 million.

The consequences of the colder temperatures that plunged civilization into the so-called Little Ice Age for several centuries after 1300 were devastating. Summers were rainy, winters cold, and in many places temperatures were too low for grain crops to mature. Famines and epidemics raged, and average life expectancy dropped by 10 years. In Germany, thousands of villages were abandoned and entire stretches of land depopulated.

The shock produced by the cold was as deep-seated it was long-lasting. When temperatures plunged unexpectedly once again in the 1960s, many meteorologists were quick to warn people about the coming of a new ice age—supposedly triggered by man-made air pollution. Hardly anyone at the time believed a warming trend could pose a threat.

The Modern Environmental Movement

It was not until the rise of the environmental movement in the 1980s that everything suddenly changed. From then on it was almost a foregone conclusion that global warming could only be perceived as a disaster for the earth's climate. Environmentalists, adopting a strategy typical of the Catholic Church, have been warning us about the horrors of greenhouse gas hell ever since—painting it as a punishment for the sin of meddling with creation. What was conveniently ignored, however, is that humanity has been reshaping the planet for a very long time, first by clearing forests and plowing fields, and later by building roads, cities and factories.

Some environmentalists doubt that the large-scale extinction of animals and plants some have predicted will in fact come about.

In the age of climate change, it has become a popular social pastime to scour the weather forecast for omens of doom. Has it ever been as hot in April as it is this year? Is this lack of rain normal? Could all this mean that the end is nigh?

Nowadays hardly anyone dares to question the increasingly shrill warnings about our climate, as more and more people jump on the hand-wringing bandwagon. United Nations Secretary General Ban Ki-moon, for example, recently said that climate change poses at least as big a danger to the world as war. German Chancellor Angela Merkel agrees, calling developments "more than alarming," and asking: "Are we willing to accept the fact that we now have completely unprecedented weather phenomena, such as tropical nights in the Harz (Mountains) region?" The fact that tropical nights, as every meteorologist knows, are nothing new in Germany—every summer has always had a few—seems to have escaped her attention.

The Winners and Losers of Climate Change

The apocalyptic mood seems to grow each time the United Nation's Intergovernmental Panel on Climate Change (IPCC) releases a new section of its climate change report. Climate hysteria appears to be more contagious than a flu epidemic. "We only have 13 years left to save the earth," screamed a recent front-page headline in the German tabloid *Bild*. "If mankind is unable to stop the greenhouse effect by the year 2020, it will bring about its own demise—and a horribly tortured one at that."

But how bad is climate change really? Will global warming trigger plagues of Biblical proportions? Can we look forward to endless droughts and catastrophic floods?

Or will Arrhenius end up being right after all? Could rising temperatures lead to higher crop yields and more tourism in many places? In other words, is humanity actually creating new paradises?

The truth is probably somewhere between these two extremes. Climate change will undoubtedly have losers—but it will also have winners. There will be a reshuffling of climate zones on earth. And there is something else that we can already say with certainty: The end of the world isn't coming any time soon.

Scientific Controversy

Largely unnoticed by the public, climate researchers are currently embroiled in their own struggle over who owns the truth. While some have always seen themselves as environmental activists aiming to shake humanity out of its complacency, others argue for a calmer and more rational approach to the unavoidable.

One member of the levelheaded camp is Hans von Storch, 57, a prominent climate researcher who is director of the Institute for Coastal Research at the GKSS Research Center in Geesthacht in northern Germany. "We have to take away people's fear of climate change," Storch told *Der Spiegel* in a recent interview. "Unfortunately many scientists see themselves too much as priests whose job it is to preach moralistic sermons to people."

Keeping a cool head is a good idea because, for one thing, we can no longer completely prevent climate change. No matter how much governments try to reduce carbon dioxide emissions, it will only be possible to limit the rise in global temperatures to about 2 degrees Celsius (3.6 degrees Fahrenheit) by the end of the century. But even this moderate warming would likely have far fewer apocalyptic consequences than many a prophet of doom would have us believe.

For one thing, the more paleontologists and geologists study the history of the earth's climate, the more clearly do they recognize just how much temperatures have fluctuated in both directions in the past. Even major fluctuations appear to be completely natural phenomena.

Additionally, some environmentalists doubt that the large-scale extinction of animals and plants some have predicted will in fact come about. "A warmer climate helps promote species diversity," says Munich zoologist Josef Reichholf.

Also, more detailed simulations have allowed climate researchers to paint a considerably less dire picture than in the past—gone is the talk of giant storms, the melting of the Antarctic ice shield and flooding of major cities.

Diverse Benefits Around the World

Improved regionalized models also show that climate change can bring not only drawbacks, but also significant benefits, especially in northern regions of the world where it has been too cold and uncomfortable for human activity to flourish in the past. However it is still a taboo to express this idea in public.

For example, countries like Canada and Russia can look forward to better harvests and a blossoming tourism industry, and the only distress the Scandinavians will face is the guilty conscience that could come with benefiting from global warming.

There is no doubt that there will be droughts in other parts of the world, especially in subtropical regions. But the widespread assumption that it is developing countries—that is, the world's poor—who will, as always, be the ones to suffer is incorrect. According to current predictions, precipitation in large parts of Africa will hardly decrease at all, except in the southern part of the continent. In fact, these same forecasts show the Sahel, traditionally a region beset by drought and famine, actually becoming wetter.

By contrast, some wealthy industrialized nations—in fact, those principally responsible for climate change—will likely face growing problems related to drought. The world's new drought zones lie in the southern United States and Australia, but also in Mediterranean countries like Spain, Italy and Greece.

How Will Europe Be Affected?

All of this will lead to a major shift within Europe, potentially leading to tough times for southern Spain's mega-resorts and boom times for hotels along the North Sea and Baltic Sea coasts. While the bulk of summer vacationers will eventually lose interest in roasting on Spain's Costa del Sol, Mediterranean conditions could prevail between the German North Sea island of Sylt and Bavaria's Lake Starnberg. The last few weeks of spring in Germany offered a taste of what's to come, as sun-loving crowds packed Berlin's urban beach bars and Munich's beer gardens.

The predicted temperature increase of 3 degrees Celsius would mean that summers in Hamburg, not far from the North Sea coast, would be as warm as they are today in the southwestern city of Freiburg, while conditions in Freiburg would be more like those in Marseille today. Germany will undoubtedly be one of the beneficiaries of climate change. Perhaps palm trees will be growing on the island of Helgoland in the North Sea soon, and German citizens will be saving billions in heating costs—which in turn would lead to a reduction in CO_2 emissions.

But climate change will also have its drawbacks. While German summers will be less rainy, fall and winter rainfall in the country's north will increase by up to 30 percent—and snow will be a thing of the past. Heavy downpours will also become more common. To avoid flooding, steps will have to be taken to provide better drainage for fields and farmlands, as well as to restore natural flood plains.

A healthy dose of skepticism is a good idea, especially when scientists become all too confident and make themselves out to be oracles.

Meanwhile, the Kiel Institute for World Economics warns that higher temperatures could mean thousands of heat-related deaths every year. But the extrapolations that lead to this dire prediction are based on the mortality rate in the unusually hot summer of 2003, for which Germans were wholly unprepared. But if hot summer days do become the norm, people will simply adjust by taking siestas and installing air-conditioning.

The medical benefits of higher average temperatures have also been ignored. According to Richard Tol, an environmental economist, "warming temperatures will mean that in 2050 there will be about 40,000 fewer deaths in Germany attributable to cold-related illnesses like the flu."

Examining Climate Myths

Another widespread fear about global warming—that it will cause super-storms that could devastate towns and villages with unprecedented fury—also appears to be unfounded. Current long-term simulations, at any rate, do not suggest that such a trend will in fact materialize.

"According to our computer model, neither the number nor intensity of storms is increasing," says Jochem Marotzke, director of the Hamburg-based Max Planck Institute for Meteorology, one of the world's leading climate research centers. "Only the boundaries of low-pressure zones are changing slightly, meaning that weather is becoming more severe in Scandinavia and less so in the Mediterranean."

According to another persistent greenhouse legend, massive flooding will strike major coastal cities, raising horrific scenarios of New York, London and Shanghai sinking into the tide. However this horror story is a relic of the late 1980s, when climate simulations were far less precise than they are today. At the time, some experts believed that the Antarctic ice shield could melt, which would in fact lead to a dramatic 60-meter (197-foot) rise in sea levels. The nuclear industry quickly seized upon and publicized the scenario, which it recognized as an argument in favor of its emissions-free power plants.

But it quickly became apparent that the horrific tale of a melting South Pole was nothing but fiction. The average temperature in the Antarctic is -30 degrees Celsius. Humanity cannot possibly burn enough oil and coal to melt this giant block of ice. On the contrary, current climate models suggest that the Antarctic will even increase in mass: Global warming will cause more water to evaporate, and part of that moisture will fall as snow over Antarctica, causing the ice shield to grow. As a result, the total rise in sea levels would in fact be reduced by about 5 cm (2 inches).

It's a different story in the warmer regions surrounding the North Pole. According to an American study published last week, the Arctic could be melting even faster than previously assumed. But because the Arctic sea ice already floats in the water, its melting will have virtually no effect on sea levels.

There's Time Left to Take Action

Nevertheless, sea levels will rise worldwide as higher temperatures cause the water in the oceans to expand. In addition, more water will flow into the ocean with the gradual thawing of the Greenland ice sheet. All things considered, however, in the current IPCC report climatologists are predicting a rise in sea levels of only about 40 centimeters (16 inches)—compared with the previous estimate of about one meter (more than three feet). A 40-centimeter rise in sea levels will hardly result in more catastrophic flooding. "We have more computer models and better ones today, and the prognoses have become more precise as a result," explains Peter Lemke of the Alfred Wegener Institute for Polar and Marine Research in the northern German port city of Bremerhaven.

Some researchers do, however, estimate that regional effects could produce an 80-centimeter (31-inch) rise in the sea level along Germany's North Sea coast. This will lead to higher storm surges—a problem the local population, already accustomed to severe weather, could easily address by building taller dikes.

Another comforting factor—especially for poorer countries like Bangladesh—is that none of these changes will happen overnight, but gradually over several decades. "We still have enough time to react," says Storch.

In short, the longer researchers allow their supercomputers to crunch the numbers, the more does the expected deluge dissipate. A rise in sea levels of several meters could only occur if Greenland were largely ice-free, but this is something scientists don't expect to happen for at least a few more centuries or even millennia. This lengthy timeframe raises the question of whether the current prognoses are even reliable.

Unknown Factors

A healthy dose of skepticism is a good idea, especially when scientists become all too confident and make themselves out to be oracles. But there can be a wide gap between their predictions and the end result—a fundamental weakness of all computer simulations that present only incomplete pictures of reality.

In the early years, for example, computer modelers underestimated the influence of aerosols, especially the sulfur particles that are released into the atmosphere during the combustion of oil and coal or during volcanic eruptions. These pollution particles block sunlight and thus cause significant cooling. The failure to adequately take aerosols into account explains why earlier models predicted a more drastic rise in temperatures than those in use today. One major unknown in the predictions depends on how quickly countries like China will filter out the pollutants from their power plant emissions—if the air becomes cleaner it will also heat up more rapidly.

Other factors that can either weaken or strengthen the greenhouse effect are still not fully understood today. For example, will the carbon dioxide trapped in the world's oceans be released as the water heats up, thereby accelerating global warming? And how much faster do land plants and sea algae grow in a milder climate? Plant proliferation could bind more carbon dioxide—and serve to slow down the greenhouse effect.

But the main problem lies in correctly calculating the effects of clouds. The tops of clouds act as mirrors in the sky, reflecting sunlight back into space—thus cooling the planet. But the bottom sides keep the heat radiated by the earth from escaping into the atmosphere—causing temperatures to rise.

Which of the two effects predominates depends primarily on the altitude at which clouds form. Simply put, low clouds tend to promote cooling while high clouds increase warming. So far scientists agree on only one thing, namely that more clouds will form in a greenhouse climate. They just don't know at which altitude.

Even the most powerful computer models are still too imprecise to simulate the details. However, the clouds alone will determine whether temperatures will increase by one degree more or less than the average predicted by the models. This is a significant element of uncertainty. "Clouds are still our biggest headache," concedes Erich Roeckner of the Max Planck Institute for Meteorology.

Roeckner is a conscientious man and a veteran of climate research, so he, of all people, should know the limits of simulation programs. Roeckner, who constantly expects surprises, neatly sums up the problem when he says: "No model will ever be as complex as nature."

3

Climate Change Will Force the Relocation of Communities

Marwaan Macan-Markar

Marwaan Macan-Markar is a journalist.

Island communities are feeling intense pressure because of climate change. The Pacific island nation of Tuvalu, for instance, has seen its agricultural land become salinized and its beaches disappear because of rising sea levels, and thousands of the island's inhabitants are facing the prospect of leaving their homeland. While some governments have been receptive to taking in refugees, the larger issue is that the problems faced in Tuvalu may soon be seen on other islands. This development could create a new class of refugees: those forced from their homes because of climate change. While there is a growing international acceptance of the problem of rising sea levels, little of substance has yet been done to stem the damage.

A rapidly warming planet may soon create a new class of refugees—those fleeing climate change in their homelands.

Tuvalu is showing signs of such a dire prospect. The Pacific island nation of some 12,000 people has already appealed to the governments of Australia and New Zealand to open their doors for its citizens to find a new home, states a background note by the secretariat of United Nations Framework Convention on Climate Change (UNFCCC).

Marwaan Macan-Markar, "Climate Change: Wanted—Homes for Small Island People," IPS/InterPress Service, April 3, 2008. Reproduced by permission.

Why New Homes Are Needed

The appeal stems from the Polynesian island "witnessing the salinisation of agricultural land and vanishing beaches due to sea-level rise," adds the note. The Tuvaluan government wants to find new homes "for at least 3,000 people, and possibly its whole population, within the next few years".

So far, the New Zealand government has been receptive, says Ian Fry, international environmental officer in Tuvalu's ministry of natural resources and lands. "The New Zealand government has approved a limited intake of about 17 people a year. The Australian government has rejected the appeal."

But Tuvalu hopes to make another appeal to Canberra later this year [2008], Fry said in an interview. "Climate change has become a security issue for us; the security of an entire nation is being threatened by global warming. Tuvalu may be uninhabitable in 30 years if there is no global action to stop the sea-level rising."

The world's major polluters cannot afford to ignore this growing problem that one day will produce climate change refugees.

In fact, Tuvalu's predicament is shared by island-nations that belong to a 38-member bloc, the Small Island Developing States (SIDS). And for this group, the week-long climate change talks in Bangkok has offered another platform to raise the alarm about their survival if the world fails to drastically cut greenhouse gas (GhG) emissions, and if there is no aid to help the SIDS adapt to the ravages of climate change.

"We are the first group of countries directly affected by climate change. For us, the talks here are more than simply addressing economic issues; it is about our existence," Selwin Hart, the SIDS coordinator, told IPS. "Our role at meetings of the UNFCCC has been unique. We have always served as the conscience of the climate change convention."

How Governments Can Help

The Bangkok meeting, which runs from Mar. 31 to Apr. 4 [2008], has attracted over 1,100 climate-change negotiators from 163 countries to discuss a new international pact that aims reduce global warming and to help developing countries adapt to a green-friendly development culture. These are the first round of talks following a major U.N. climate change conference held last December [2007] in Bali, where a deal was struck between the developing and developed world to shape a global response against a rapidly heating planet.

The 1992 Convention on Climate Change was endorsed by 192 countries at the Earth Summit in Rio de Janeiro as a response to warnings by the scientific community that rapid GhG emissions would wreck the health of the planet. In 1997, a new treaty, the Kyoto Protocol, was added to strengthen the UNFCCC. It mandated the industrialised nations to slash, as a first step, GhG emissions by 5 percent by 2012.

And what SIDS wants through the climate change talks is a course of action that will help its members to avoid the plight of Tuvalu. "We want to avoid moving to a foreign country. We are trying to address this problem before it becomes an issue beyond our control," Pasha Carruthers, head of the Cook Islands delegation at the Bangkok talks, told IPS. "Projects for us to adapt are essential if SIDS are to be viable."

Green groups from the Pacific Ocean islands agree. "There is growing awareness among communities about the uncertain future. There are issues being addressed by some of the local churches," says Arieta Moceica, climate advisor for Greenpeace in Suva, Fiji. "But to move from their island will not be easy. It will mean loss of their culture, their identity and way of life."

Yet conferences being held under the UNFCCC are still to openly embrace the unique concerns of the SIDS, she admitted in an interview. "It is time that the link between climate change and human rights be recognised at these talks. The world's major polluters cannot afford to ignore this growing problem that one day will produce climate change refugees."

A Human Rights Issue

For now, though, help has come from another quarter. In late March, the Geneva-based U.N. Human Rights Council acknowledged, for the first time, that climate change could undermine the human rights of people living in small island states, coastal areas and in areas of the world hit by harsh weather, such as severe droughts and floods.

This new milestone in the world's human rights landscape was due to the dogged diplomatic efforts of countries like Maldives and Tuvalu. It comes over two decades after the leader of the Indian Ocean island made a moving speech at the U.N. The "Death of a Nation" speech delivered in 1987 awakened the world to the plight of small islands threatened by rising sea levels.

"Since then, we have always highlighted our vulnerability due to global warming," says Amjad Abdulla, director general of the Maldives' environment, energy and water ministry. "The basic argument is that vulnerable communities have a right to exist. We have tried to draw attention to the human dimension of climate change."

Yet despite such appeals, progress under the UNFCCC has been minimal, he told IPS. "We are very disappointed at the slow implementation of the Kyoto Protocol. We can't watch and see things happen to our countries. This is a scary thing."

4

Climate Change Affects the Natural World

Ker Than

Ker Than is a staff writer for Space.com and LiveScience.

Recent changes in habitat have been observed in the animal world. From fish species migrating north in search of cooler water to marmots coming out of hibernation weeks earlier than in the past, animals are showing that their environments are being significantly affected at a faster rate than scientists expected. It is possible that climate change could reduce diversity in the animal world, as human development disrupts the timing of natural events and affects animal growth and behavior.

The planet is warming, humans are mostly to blame and plants and animals are going to dramatic lengths to cope. That's the consensus of a number of recent studies that used wildlife to gauge the extent of global warming and its effects.

As humans argue about thermometer readings, animals are providing evidence that should be figured in to scientific and political decisions.

While the topic of climate change is contentious—including whether the planet is actually heating up—a growing number of documented shifts in traits and behaviors in the wild kingdom is leading many scientists to conclude the world is changing in unnatural ways.

Among the changes:

- Marmots end their hibernations about three weeks earlier now compared to 30 years ago.

- Polar bears today are thinner and less healthy than those of 20 years ago.

- Many fish species are moving northward in search of cooler waters.

- A fruitfly gene normally associated with hot, dry conditions has spread to populations living in traditionally cooler southern regions.

Scientific Argument, Natural Facts

Over the past century, Earth's average temperature has risen by about 1 degree Fahrenheit and many scientists believe greenhouse gases and carbon dioxide emissions from human activities are to blame. Left unattended, they warn, temperatures may rise by an additional 2–10 degrees by the end of the century. In the leading computer models, it follows that polar ice will melt and seas would rise drastically, threatening coastal communities around the globe.

A handful of scientists dispute the data. Others say humans aren't to blame.

Terry Root, an environmental science and policy professor at Stanford University, says that as humans argue about thermometer readings, animals are providing evidence that should be figured in to scientific and political decisions.

Global warming can reduce genetic diversity by affecting the connections between species populations.

Animals are "just reacting to what's going on out there," Root says. "And if their behavior is very similar to what we expect with what's going on with global warming—if they're shifting and they're moving, if they're changing their breeding time by 5 days in 10 years—we can use that information to support what the thermometers are also showing."

Climate change can occur naturally, but what worries many scientists the most—and the reason why they don't think this is part of a natural cycle—is the rapid rate at which the current changes are happening—changes that are being reflected in the responses of wildlife.

Divide and Destroy

In a 2003 study published in the journal *Nature*, Root and her colleagues analyzed numerous studies involving wild plant and animals for changes due to global warming. Out of the nearly 1,500 species examined, the researchers found that about 1,200 exhibited temperature-related changes consistent with what scientists would expect if they were being affected by global warming.

The authors highlighted four possible ways that species might respond to rising temperatures, all of which have been documented by other studies and researchers.

The first is for species to migrate northward or move to higher elevations. The ubiquitous presence of humans, however, is making this option difficult for some species.

"The thing that is very, very different from prehistoric times is that there are now K-Mart parking lots these species have to cross as they try to move north to get away from the heat down south" Root told *LiveScience*.

As a result, species that can't adapt to urban or agricultural environments become isolated, their lines of retreat cut off.

In a study published last year in the journal *PLoS Biology*, Elizabeth Hadly, a biologist at Stanford University, examined fossil records from past warming periods and concluded that global warming can reduce genetic diversity by affecting the connections between species populations.

The best way to ensure species survival is to have large, interconnected populations that are genetically diverse, Hadly explained in an email interview.

This means that even if the genetic diversity of a species as a whole is high, if the individuals are scattered and prevented from interbreeding, they can become just as vulnerable to disease and external threats as a species with a *small* population and *low* genetic diversity. Like the military strategy of divide-and-conquer, a group that together might have had the resources to withstand an assault can be picked off one by one if split up.

Connections among individuals within a species aren't the only things that can be disrupted: global warming can also threaten the ties that bind members of *different* species to one another.

Many biologists, including [Charles] Darwin, once believed that species responded to temperature changes as a group, thus preserving their relationships to one another. But scientists are finding that this is often not the case.

Instead, different species respond to environmental stressors in different ways, and this can lead to what Root calls the "tearing apart of communities."

Global warming is going to be a big stress to all animals, including Homo sapiens.

Intricate Connections

The second prediction was that the timing of natural events like flowering, migration, and egg-laying could shift. Ecosystems are intricately connected webs, and even if a species doesn't rely on temperature and daylight cues to trigger certain behaviors, it may interact with other species that do.

"Thousands of years of co-evolution could easily be disrupted," Root says.

Third, the body size and behaviors of species may change in response to rising temperatures. For example, scientists believe that as a general rule, bodies become smaller in response to general warming and larger with cooling.

A 2003 study led by Philip Gingerich, a geological sciences professor at the University of Michigan, looked at horse fossils from a warming period that occurred 55 million years ago. They found that as temperatures rose, the fossils shrank, from the size of a small dog to a house cat. The researchers believed the dwarfing might have resulted from the horses eating plants whose tissues were low in protein but high in toxic compounds—plants that flourished in the carbon dioxide-rich environment of the time.

Finally, species can undergo genetic changes. This last prediction has been documented in at least two species, the red squirrel and the fruitfly *Drosophila*.

Business as Usual?

Not all scientists are convinced humans have anything to do with climate change or the shifts seen in the animal world.

Patrick Michaels, an environmental science professor at the University of Virginia, believes the current warming is part of a natural cycle.

"It's what you'd expect," Michaels told *LiveScience*. "It's not all a result of human induced climate change. Half of it is at best, probably less than half."

"Even if humans are causing global warming," Michaels said, "there is little we can do to change it. If it is an issue, it is one that we will have to adapt to."

Patrick believes the wildlife changes are likewise natural.

"With all due respect, you would expect to see some slight changes in the distribution of plants and animals as the planet warms—or as the planet cools for that matter," Michaels said. "It's hardly newsworthy."

If anything, most species would benefit from an earlier spring, and focusing on global warming is a harmful distraction from more serious problems afflicting wildlife, Michaels says. "If you asked me which one we should worry about more—changes in climate or human-caused changes in habitat—I would say that the latter is much more important."

"Overall climate will change quite a bit," Michaels said. "However, if you change characteristics of the surface—if you turn forest into farmland—that will have more severe effects on wildlife than merely changing the temperature a degree or two."

A Stressful Future for All Species

Ecosystems and wildlife aren't the only things that increasing temperatures will affect.

"Global warming is going to be a big stress to all animals, including *Homo sapiens*," said Root.

A recent report issued by the Pew Center for Global Climate Change, a Virginia-based nonprofit organization, warned that rising temperatures could exacerbate health risks such as asthma for the elderly, the infirm and the poor, and especially for those in poor countries.

Even if all pollution were stopped today, the climate will warm at least another degree by the year 2100 and seas will rise 4 inches (11 centimeters), according to one recent study. Another report says warming is unstoppable through the year 2400. Despite the dire warnings, many scientists believe it may not be too late to reverse the trend.

The Pew report suggests creating transitional habitats that link natural areas as a way to help migrating species. Also, alleviating other environmental stressors like habitat destruction could help reduce their combined effects with global warming.

Root is encouraged by the fact that many cities are following higher environmental standards, even if state and national governments are dragging their feet.

In the end, she believes, it will be the relatively small things that people do that will have the biggest impact: "Hummer sales, thank heaven, are dropping since gas prices have gone up, and hybrid [car] sales have gone up. It's that type of stuff."

5

Indigenous Arctic Cultures Struggle to Adapt to Climate Change

Alex Shoumatoff

Alex Shoumatoff is a frequent contributor to Vanity Fair *and the author of* African Madness.

In 2007, Russia conducted an expedition to the North Pole in search of oil located in the area of arctic waters that Russia claims it owns. While the expedition sparked an international controversy over what countries can claim ownership rights to what parts of the North Pole, it raised another significant issue: the consequences of energy exploration in the area. The North Pole is already feeling the effects of climate change: ice is melting, animals are losing their homes, and indigenous cultures are struggling to adapt to the loss of their livelihoods. While the idea of drilling in the North Pole is tantalizing to many countries, the very real effects of climate change serve as a reminder of the negative consequences of climate change in this part of the world.

By some estimates, 25 percent of the world's remaining fossil-fuel reserves are buried under the Arctic Ocean. With the ice cap shrinking by 28,000 square miles a year, and gigantic pools of open water appearing as it splits, the possibility of getting at them is improving daily. Meanwhile, oil supplies are dwindling, and prices are rising to historic highs, making expensive oil exploration more and more worthwhile. . . .

Alex Shoumatoff, "The Arctic Oil Rush," *Vanity Fair*, May 2008. Reproduced by permission.

The new accessibility of the Arctic's deposits is not going to make the effort to curb global warming any easier. Ironically, fossil-fuel emissions are making more fossil fuel available. It's as if someone on the verge of bankruptcy were suddenly to get a huge inheritance from a distant relative he didn't even know. Compounding this vicious circle is another feedback loop that is making the top of the planet warm twice as fast as anywhere else: as more bare land and open water are exposed by melting, more solar heat is absorbed instead of being reflected back by white ice and snow. With global warming already stressing the Arctic's animals and its million or so indigenous people, its newfound wealth could be the *coup de grâce.* . . .

Dividing Up the Arctic

I catch a cab to the Russian Institute of Geography, which is on a side street in Old Moscow, in a building that used to be a poorhouse during the time of Ivan the Terrible and whose ratty décor is still U.S.S.R. 1960. Nikolai Osokin, a glaciologist who has been studying the Arctic's shifting ice for 45 years and is an authority on its fossil-fuel deposits, shows me the line that Stalin drew from Murmansk to the pole to the middle of the Bering Sea in 1926, which he declared to be the limits of the Russian Arctic. It is still in post-Soviet atlases, and no one, Osokin says, has ever disputed it. Canada had similarly defined its Arctic territory, shooting lines from its eastern- and westernmost points to the pole a year earlier. "Traditionally, all the Arctic countries mention their own sectors," Osokin says. "Only in the last 10 years is the discussion about unfairness of definition of sectors." This is how the seven countries with claims in Antarctica divvied up the continent in 1959, agreeing not to use their sectors for military purposes or to exploit their resources until 2048. (The claims had been asserted in the first half of the 20th century, beginning with Britain—on the basis of its disputed ownership of the Falkland Islands and its explorations, going back to Captain John Strong in 1690—and followed by France, Norway, Argentina, Chile, Australia, and New Zealand.)

Many feel the best thing for the Arctic would be a similar arrangement. The ships that pass through the Arctic Ocean could be taxed by an international body, and the proceeds could be used to help the indigenous people and wildlife, whose eco-system and livelihoods are melting from under them. . . .

"Drunken forests," whose trees slant every which way, because the roots have lost their purchase in the liquefying, buckling soil, are becoming increasingly common.

Changes in Siberia

I fly to Yakutsk, in far-eastern Siberia, six time zones ahead of Moscow. Yakutsk is the capital of Yakutia, or, more correctly, the Sakha Autonomous Republic, which is as big as India but has only a million people, instead of a billion. In that region, the permafrost, the layer of permanently frozen soil that covers as much as 25 percent of the earth's land, is the deepest in the world, a mile and a half thick in the Viliui River basin. The Lomonosov Ridge shoots off to the pole from close to the New Siberian Islands, in the Laptev Sea, above Yakutia. The coldest confirmed temperature in the Northern Hemisphere—minus 67.8 degrees Celsius—was recorded in Verkhoyansk, which is also the oldest European settlement in the Arctic. I want to go there and look for mammoth tusks that are being heaved up by the melting permafrost, a welcome development for the again-flourishing ivory market. Woolly mammoths were hairy pachyderms that died out during the last big warming event, 10,000 years ago. Their tusks, nearly circular (while those of modern elephants have a more gradual curve), are also made of ivory, and are turning up with increasing frequency in Hong Kong and in mainland China.

I also want to meet some of the Yakut horse breeders, whose traditional lifestyle is being threatened by the great thaw. They and the other native people of the Yakut Arctic—the Yukaghir and the Eveny and Evenki reindeer herders—have powerful shamans, although only a handful are left. Some are said to be able to drum themselves into a trance and become winged reindeer, flying up into the sky to see where the game is.

The shamans have been persecuted since czarist times, as devil worshippers by the Orthodox priests, and as enemies of the people by the Soviets, who threw them out of helicopters, saying, "You want to fly? Here's your chance." Animism is the main religion in Yakutia. Three-quarters of the people still live close to nature, attuned to the animals and plants, and are acutely aware of the changes that are occurring because of the mild temperatures.

You don't have to be a shaman to see what is happening to the tundra; it's visible from the plane window. The tundra is pitted with circular depressions known as "alases." Some of them are filled with water from the thawing permafrost; some are empty craters from which the meltwater has drained as it found new exits in the iceless soil. The "thermokarst lakes," as the water-filled ones are called, are bubbling with methane that had been trapped in the ice. Methane is at least 20 times more powerful a greenhouse gas than carbon dioxide. (The Siberian permafrost zone alone contains an estimated 500 gigatons of carbon. The entire annual human output is about five and a half gigatons.)

No one knows how much methane is being released, because we don't yet have the capability for "spot" measurement, Corell tells me. But it's a ticking time bomb, enough to turn the world into a cauldron, should it all get into the atmosphere.

Only about 10 percent of Yakutia, however, is methane-emitting tundra. Most of it is taiga, forest dominated by larch trees, which are taking carbon out of the atmosphere, so the tundra and the taiga more or less balance each other out. The taiga is spreading north with the rising temperature, pushing the tundra to the edge of the Laptev Sea, forcing migrating cranes and geese to relocate their historic summer nesting sites. "Drunken forests," whose trees slant every which way, because the roots have lost their purchase in the liquefying, buckling soil, are becoming increasingly common. . . .

Don't take from nature more than you need; if you take more, you are not respecting nature. But all our economic basis now is to take more and more.

Shrinking Reindeer Herds

The Eveny and Evenki people (same way of life, different linguistic heritage) have been relying for centuries on reindeer (known in the Nearctic as caribou), which provide transport, food, shelter, and clothing. There are still a few thousand nomadic reindeer herders in Siberia, moving with their animals in the largest territory of any remaining traditional people. But the wild and domesticated reindeer have been experiencing massive die-offs in the spring and fall, I'm told by Eveny and Evenki activists. Reindeer eat mainly lichen, and now when the seasons change there is more rain that freezes at night, often with melted snow, into a sheet of ice that the reindeer can't break through with their hooves, so entire herds are starving to death.

Vyacheslav Shadrin, the head of the council of Yukaghir elders, tells me that in the Upper Kolyma basin, 700 miles north of Yakutsk, where he is from, last November and December, when it is normally minus 40 degrees Celsius (also Fahrenheit—Celsius and Fahrenheit converge at 40 below), it rained. That means it was 72 degrees Fahrenheit warmer than usual. The Yukaghir are one of the oldest aboriginal peoples of Siberia. There are only 1,509 of them left, as of the last census, and only 23 who still speak the language fluently. They are a culture on the way out, unless something is done fast to keep it going.

Losing More Than Income

The Upper Kolyma Yukaghir are hunters and fishermen whose main source of income is trapping sable. "Usually in one season a hunter can get 20 to 25 pelts, half of them in the middle of October, when the sables all go to their winter hunting ground," Shadrin says. "By then the snow comes thick and the lakes are frozen and the hunters can go out to the winter routes on snowmobiles. But now it's no longer safe to go out until mid-November, because the snowmobiles can fall through the ice, so the hunters are losing the most important month and a half for their income.

"Every year the pasture for the wild reindeer, which the Yukaghir hunt, is getting less and less because the taiga is coming up from the south," Shadrin goes on. "Grasses, birches, and some bushes like willow are covering the lichen. And the reindeer no longer come to their traditional river crossings, which is the best place to kill them. The hunters no longer know where they are going to be, so they lose time and are less successful.

"The quantity of wolves is growing," he says. "Before, we used to have only tundra wolves. Now we're getting taiga wolves, too, which run in bigger packs. The wolves kill many reindeer and give trouble to the herders. So for all these reasons, both wild and domestic reindeer are disappearing. Also, geese and sea ducks have changed their migratory routes and schedules. Hunters used to wait for them where they rested at night in the beginning of June; now they don't know what time to go. Last few years the waterfowl have been appearing in very small quantity. They must have changed their route to another river basin. Trapping polar foxes was a big part of our traditional life, but in the last 10 or 15 years there have hardly been any. No one knows why.

"Now the runoff from the breakup of the ice and snow is greater, every spring water comes more, and there is more danger from flooding and erosion to our villages, which are all on the riverbanks. At the same time, some of our best lakes for fishing are disappearing." These must be thermokarst lakes being drained by new subterranean streams in the thawing permafrost.

Shadrin continues: "Polar bears are coming into Cherskiy [a town near the mouth of the Kolyma River]. Usually at the end of summer, when the ice pack is melting, the pregnant bears come to the land to have their cubs, and afterward, with the small bears, they return to the ice and spend the winter hunting seals. The ice used to be a short swim from the shore, but now it is very far away. The bears cannot even see it, so they stay onshore and try to find food around the places where people live." By some estimates, as many as half of the world's remaining polar bears may be in Russia.

What are the old people saying about these changes?, I ask. "They're saying nature is lying to the people," Shadrin says. "It is not respecting them, because the people are doing many bad things, killing many animals, cutting many forests, many plants, dirtying rivers and lakes. They forget that they live in a natural world and are not respecting old traditions, so nature is returning to people their bad actions. One of the results of the melting is that too many mammoth bones appear on the land and people are collecting them, but in our tradition the mammoth is the spirit of the underworld and we can't take their bones. So the elders are saying we have awakened these underworld spirits. The main thesis of our traditional view is: Don't take from nature more than you need; if you take more, you are not respecting nature. But all our economic basis now is to take more and more."

Different City, Similar Difficulties

I fly up to Verkhoyansk in an old Antonov An-24, a no-nonsense piece of Soviet machinery. I'm the only non-Asian on the plane. Below is the Lena River, the world's 10th-longest, and the largest river you've never heard of. In another two months it will be frozen 15 feet thick and will become a highway for trucks and jeeps. We fly over the snow-covered Verkhoyansk Range and touch down at Batagay, a charmless outpost of three-story barracks built in the 1930s. It's raining and overcast. The next five days will be like being in a grainy black-and-white movie. My driver Sergei and I set out down a road built by gulag prisoners through the endless expanse of golden larch. This was the gulag [Soviet Union-era camps for political prisoners] heartland. The camps had no walls, because escape was impossible; there was nowhere to escape to. . . .

A cozy burg of 1,800 which has been having a rough time since the end of Soviet subsidizing of remote rural communities, Verkhoyansk was founded in 1638 by Cossacks sent out by Czar Mikhail I to conquer the surrounding region. It's on the Yana River, which flows into the Laptev Sea, and is older than St. Petersburg. Many early explorers, including Vitus Bering in the early 18th century, passed through here. "The prisoners did a lot for our town," the mayor, Pyotor Gabyshev, tells me. "They introduced potatoes and cucumbers. One of them did the first ethnography of the Yakut, which the Yakut themselves, who have forgotten many of their ceremonies, now consult. They built a meteorological station, which in 1892 recorded the temperature of minus 67.8 Celsius. But now even 55 below has become very rare. Before, it would drizzle for 10 days straight. Now there are hard rains, which are more destructive. People are hunting for freshly exposed mammoth bones for extra income." He gives me a certificate stating that I have been to the Pole of Cold.

The next morning I go to a camp of traditional Yakut horse breeders. The Yakut, or Sakha, were mounted warriors who arrived a few centuries before the Cossacks and conquered the reindeer herders and the Yukaghir, and were in turn subjugated by the Cossacks. . . .

The bank [of the Yana River] and the bone-filled permafrost behind it are undergoing active, rapid disintegration.

The horse-breeding camp is 15 minutes down the Yana by motorboat, then a 15-minute slog through the muddy taiga. There are three huts with flat tops and slanted walls, where two breeders, three haymakers, and an old man who is supposed to have clairvoyant powers are living and taking care of 130 horses—the hardy native Yana-Indigirka breed, which is thought to be close to the original horse. Everyone is feasting on Arctic hares and *tuganok*, small white fish from the river. Braces of freshly shot white hares hang from the rafters. This is the time of year when every able-bodied person in the region is hunting hares. I will eat almost nothing my whole time in the Arctic but hare and sour cream so thick you can stand a spoon in it.

There is a local cycle of 10 years of rain, followed by 10 dry years, the old man, whose name is Zachar, tells me. We are in the fifth year of the rainy cycle. Spring is coming weeks earlier, and winter weeks later, Zachar says. Strange birds are appearing, ones that have never been seen in the region, and a little deer called the *kosulya* has just shown up from central Yakutia. "I don't know where the cold has gone. Maybe to the other side of the planet, where you live." Afraid not, I say. In another month these six men will be on their own, living on pike, duck, and moose. "This is a dying way of life," Leonid, who owns the herd, tells me. "It's hard to find strong young men who are willing to spend the winter in such isolation anymore."

On the way back to the river, we see, sitting on a pond in a bog, one of the ducks that weren't here before, a gray *selezen*, with greenish tail feathers. All kinds of animals and plants are moving up into Yakutia, whose biodiversity has increased across the board except for reptiles and amphibians. If this seems like a silver lining, it is not good news for the Arctic species. And while the active permafrost layer may not be getting any deeper, after a few days of steady rain it has become a muddy soup. Our jeep gets stuck and it takes an hour of prying with pine logs to get it out. . . .

In the morning we head down the extravagantly meandering Yana in a motorboat until we come to where the river is maybe half a mile wide and the gently curving bank rises from 20 feet high to more than 100 for a mile and a half. The place is called Ulakhan Suullur and is a famous cemetery for mammoths and other Pleistocene mega-fauna, including woolly rhinos, musk oxen, and cave lions. The most popular theory is that it was a swamp thousands of years ago when the last ice age was coming to an end, and the big mammals got stuck in its mud. The mammoth was basically done in by climate change. The last ones survived on Wrangel Island, north of Chukotka, until 3,700 years ago. According to Eveny mythology, mammoths scooped up dirt with their tusks to form the first dry land. . . .

Two fishermen, on the way home with a sack full of 20-pound taimens, pull up. One of them spots a fresh yellow bone sticking out halfway up the bank and climbs up to get it. It's not a mammoth tusk, but the femur of a giant deer or horse. It's still heavy, having just been washed out of the solid wall of fossil ice—with ancient carcasses frozen in it like flies in amber—that is visible in places where the bank has just collapsed. The bank and the bone-filled permafrost behind it are undergoing active, rapid disintegration. Face-to-face with such a vast slice of time, my individual life seems like a mote, not even a hiccup. Our hunter-gatherer ancestors who roamed the earth 10,000 years ago hunted these massive mammals, but we were still very low on the totem pole. We've come a very long way in just the last 10,000 years—maybe to the end.

6

Climate Change Must Be Addressed in Developing Countries

ScienceDaily

ScienceDaily is an online magazine focused on science, technology, and medicine.

It is likely that Asia will experience food and water shortages unless action is taken to curb the levels of greenhouse gas emissions, according to a 2007 report from the Intergovernmental Panel on Climate Change (IPCC). The IPCC estimates that, among other dire consequences, grain yield could decrease, water availability will decline, and biodiversity will be threatened in a number of Asian countries, including Bangladesh, India, and Vietnam. The IPCC suggests that if public food distribution, disaster preparedness, and health care systems are improved, Asia's vulnerability to disasters caused by climate change could be reduced.

Food and water shortages are likely to increase in Asia unless action is taken to curb the rise in greenhouse gases, according to the Intergovernmental Panel on Climate Change (IPCC). Increasing temperatures and extreme weather patterns are already taking their toll on crop yields, which are declining in many parts of the Continent.

Future climate change is expected to put close to 50 million extra people at risk of hunger by 2020, rising to an addi-

ScienceDaily, "IPCC Report: Millions at Risk of Hunger and Water Stress in Asia Unless Global Greenhouse Emissions Cut," April 11, 2007. Reproduced by permission. http://www.sciencedaily.com.

tional 132 million and 266 million by 2050 and 2080 respectively, says the report of IPCC Working Group II.

Indeed temperatures could rise by up to five degrees C [Celsius] by 2080 unless emissions are decisively reduced, the report adds. It suggests that a 2°C increase in mean air temperature could decrease rain-fed rice yields by 5 to 12% in China and under one scenario net cereal production in South Asian countries is projected to decline by 4 to 10% by the end of this century. In Bangladesh, production of rice may fall by just under ten per cent and wheat by a third by the year 2050.

Achim Steiner, Executive Director of the United Nations Environment Programme (UNEP), which is a co-founder of the IPCC, said: "Unchecked climate change will be an environmental and economic catastrophe, but above all it will be a human tragedy. Seven of the world's most populous countries are located in Asia and future population growth over the next 50 years is projected to increase India, Pakistan and Bangladesh's populations by 570 million, 200 million and 130 million respectively."

Nearly half of Asia's biodiversity is at risk because of climate change.

"It is absolutely vital that international action is taken now to avoid dangerous climate change. Otherwise the consequences for food and water security in Asia, as for many other parts of the world, are too alarming to contemplate," he added.

"Action however cannot be confined to curbing greenhouse gases. Some level of climate change is inevitable as a result of pollution already in the atmosphere. Therefore action is also needed at the national level to mainstream 'climate proofing' into all areas of economic life so that countries and communities in the region have a chance to adapt and thus a chance to avoid some of the more extreme impacts," said Mr Steiner.

The Importance of Water

Water stress is cited as one of the most pressing environmental problems facing the region, particularly in South and Southeast Asia where the number of people living under water stress is expected to increase substantially. In India, "gross per capita water availability" will decline from around 1,820 cubic metres a year to as low as around 1,140 cubic metres a year in 2050.

"Freshwater availability in Central, South and East and Southeast Asia particularly in large river basins such as Changjiang is likely to decrease due to climate change, along with population growth and rising standard of living, which could adversely affect more than a billion people in Asia by the 2050s," the report stated.

Meanwhile, some regions are likely to see more frequent and heavier rainfall, including western China, the Changjiang Valley and the southeastern coast of China, the Arabian Peninsula, Bangladesh and along the western coasts of the Philippines. These could lead to severe flooding and increased risks from landslides and mud flows.

Himalayan glaciers are receding faster than in any other part of the world. Half a billion people in the Himalaya-Hindu-Kush region and a quarter billion downstream who rely on glacial melt waters could be seriously affected.

Glaciers in these areas could, at current rates of global warming, disappear altogether by 2035, if not sooner.

The current trends in glacial melt suggest that the Ganga, Indus, Brahmaputra and other rivers that criss-cross the northern Indian plain may become seasonal rivers in the near future as a consequence of climate change with important ramifications for poverty and the economies in the region.

Changing Sea Levels

Coastal populations are also vulnerable to sea level rise. The current level of sea level rise in coastal areas of Asia is reported to be between 1 to 3 mm [millimeters] annually, slightly higher than the global average.

"Projected sea level rise could flood the residences of millions of people living in the low-lying areas of South, Southeast and East Asia such as in Vietnam, Bangladesh, India and China. Even under the most conservative scenario, sea level will be about 40 cm higher than today by the end of 21st century and this is projected to increase the annual number of people flooded in coastal population from 13 million to 94 million," the report states.

Almost 60% of this increase will occur in South Asia (along coasts from Pakistan, through India, Sri Lanka and Bangladesh to Burma), while about 20% will occur in Southeast Asia specifically from Thailand to Vietnam including Indonesia and the Philippines.

This impact could be more pronounced in megacities located in megadeltas such as in Bangkok, Shanghai, and Tianjin, where natural ground subsidence [the lowering of the natural land surface] is enhanced by human activities.

Climate Change and Biodiversity

Nearly half of Asia's biodiversity is at risk because of climate change.

"Climate change is likely to affect forest expansion and migration, and exacerbate threats to biodiversity resulting from land use/cover change and population pressure in most of Asia. Marine and coastal ecosystems in Asia are likely to be affected by sea level rise and temperature increases," the report added.

Food insecurity and loss of livelihood are likely to be further exacerbated by the loss of cultivated land and nursery areas for fisheries by inundation and coastal erosion in low-lying areas of tropical Asia.

Climate Change and Health

Human health will also be adversely affected. Rising temperatures and rainfall variability had led to more climate-induced diseases and heat stress in Central, East, South and Southeast Asia.

Increases in illness and mortality resulting from diarrhoeal disease are expected in South and Southeast Asia. Warmer temperatures in coastal waters would exacerbate the abundance and/or toxicity of cholera in South Asia.

"Multiple stresses in Asia will be compounded further due to climate change. It is likely that climate change will impinge on sustainable development of most developing countries of Asia as it compounds the pressures on natural resources and the environment associated with rapid urbanization, industrialization, and economic development," the report said.

Suggestions for Adaptation

While development to a large extent is responsible for much of the greenhouse gases emitted into the atmosphere that drives climate change, development can also greatly contribute to reducing vulnerability to climate change and enhancing the adaptive capacity of vulnerable sectors. The report calls for the mainstreaming of sustainable development policies and including climate-proofing concepts in national development initiatives.

It suggests improvements in public food distribution, disaster preparedness and management, and health care systems to enhance social capital and reduce the vulnerability of developing countries of Asia to climate change.

Adaptation measures to deal with sea-level rise, potentially more intense cyclones and threats to ecosystems and biodiversity are also highly recommended.

Management options, such as better stock management and more integrated agro-ecosystems could likely improve land conditions and reduce pressures arising from climate change, the report added.

7

Developing Countries Have More Pressing Concerns Than Climate Change

Siddhartha Shome

Siddhartha Shome is a technical consultant.

A 2008 decision by the World Bank to finance a coal-fired power plant in India raised questions about the benefits of bringing electricity to citizens formerly lacking this utility, versus the potential of such a power plant to contribute to climate change through the byproducts of electric generation. But putting the dangers of climate change ahead of the dangers that currently exist for poor people—low literacy rates, class stratification, and unsafe drinking water, just to name a few—is a first-world luxury. People living in developing countries must be able to attain a basic level of material security and well-being, as well as education and economic opportunity, in order to adequately address the problems—in respect to climate change and other aspects of life—that will await all citizens of the world in the future.

Last week, *New York Times* reporter Andrew Revkin blogged about the World Bank's decision to finance a major new coal-fired power plant in India. Revkin ended his blog with a question: "Is all of this bad? If you're one of many climate scientists foreseeing calamity, yes. If you're a village kid in rural India looking for a light to read by, no."

Siddhartha Shome, "Maybe Horses Will Fly—Developing Countries and Global Warming," The Breakthrough Institute, April 15, 2008. Reproduced by permission. http//thebreakthrough.org/blog/2008/04/maybe_horses_will_fly_developi.shtml.

In response, the famed environmental writer Bill McKibben asked his own question:

"The really interesting question, to follow on the last sentence of the story, is: what if you're an Indian kid looking for a light to read by—and also living near the rising ocean, or vulnerable to the range expansion of dengue-bearing mosquitoes, or dependent on suddenly-in-question monsoonal rains."

Even if the most dire predictions about global warming come true, some of the poorest people in the world may still be better off tomorrow if they are able to enjoy some of the fruits of development.

Challenges Independent of Climate Change

McKibben may think he knows better but I think the answer for that village kid would probably be the same. Take the electricity and the light to read by and worry about malaria and monsoonal rains later. To get some idea of the problems facing people in rural India, just consider the following:

1. In India, the literacy rate is only 64%. The female literacy rate is even lower. In half the households in rural India, there is not a single female member above the age of 15 who can read or write.

2. Out of a population of one billion, more than 300 million Indians live on less than a dollar a day.

3. In India, some 400,000 children under the age of five die each year from diarrhoea caused by easily preventable factors such as poor hygiene and unsafe drinking water.

4. Indian society continues to be plagued by extreme forms of discrimination and exploitation based on the traditional caste system. There are many millions (estimates range from 40 million to 100 million) of bonded laborers (slaves) in India today, mainly belonging to the lowest castes, the Dalits.

5. There still exists widespread discrimination against women in India. Economist Amartya Sen estimates that in the developing world, due to the preference for sons over daughters, and due to the sheer neglect of women and girls, some 100 million women are simply missing.

In this scenario, how can one seriously suggest that the village kid in India should give up her hopes of prosperity, education, and health care today, in order to prevent rising ocean levels many years down the road? What would Americans do in the same situation? Or Europeans? Or human beings anywhere?

Current Problems vs. Future Questions

There are some very good reasons why people in rural India should first worry about their basic human necessities today, rather than about the long-term effects of global warming.

First, if you and your family don't have access to such things as clean water and basic health care, neither you, nor your children, nor your grandchildren may even be around long enough to witness tomorrow, making the future rise or fall of the world's oceans a moot point.

Second, the life of an educated, healthy and modestly prosperous person living in tomorrow's globally-warmed world of higher ocean levels may well be better than the poverty stricken life of an Indian villager in the pre-global-warming world. In other words, even if the most dire predictions about global warming come true, some of the poorest people in the world may still be better off tomorrow if they are able to enjoy some of the fruits of development, such as education, health care, electricity, etc.

Third, and most important, maybe horses will fly. Let me tell you an Indian story about the Mughal Emperor Akbar and his witty minister, Birbal. One day, for some reason, Akbar became very angry with Birbal, and ordered that he be beheaded. Birbal pleaded for his life, but to no avail. Then Birbal hit upon an idea. He promised Akbar that if he was spared for a year, he would make Akbar's favorite horse fly. Akbar relented, and let Birbal live. When a friend asked Birbal how he planned to make the horse fly, Birbal replied, "anything can happen in a year; Akbar can die; the horse can die; and who knows, maybe the horse will fly." In a slightly different context, what this means is that, first and foremost, human beings need to achieve a certain minimum level of material well-being and sense of security. And once this is achieved, who knows what wonders can happen. If the billions of impoverished people in the developing world can get widespread access to education, health care, and job opportunities, who knows what the unleashing of their talent and energy can achieve. Having met their basic needs, maybe they will start thinking about the environment. Maybe new ideas will burst forth. Maybe new and better energy technologies will be adopted, which will not only address global warming, but also ensure a minimum standard of living for all people everywhere. Maybe horses will fly.

As Ted Nordhaus and Michael Shellenberger put it in the book *Breakthrough*, "the satisfaction of the material needs of food and water and shelter is not an *obstacle* to but rather the *precondition for* the modern appreciation of the nonhuman world".

8

Laws Are Needed to Force Humans to Adapt

Mike Tidwell

Mike Tidwell is founder and director of the Chesapeake Climate Action Network.

During the civil rights era, Americans took decisive actions against the many forms of discrimination, which until then had been an accepted and institutionalized practice. These actions were a reaction to what was considered a national injustice, and citizens acted without being asked or coerced. Rather, they fought for change because it was the right thing to do. As the nation and world currently face an unprecedented climate crisis, people must react with equal force. It is not enough to change your life in small ways; rather, a wide-scale overhaul of how people live, work, and interact with the environment is needed, as are new laws that will help the government compel citizens to right an environmental injustice.

Strange but true: Energy-efficient light bulbs and hybrid cars are *hurting* our nation's budding efforts to fight global warming.

More precisely, every time an activist or politician hectors the public to *voluntarily* reach for a new bulb or spend extra on a Prius, ExxonMobil heaves a big sigh of relief.

Scientists now scream the news about global warming: it's already here and could soon, very soon, bring tremendous

Mike Tidwell, "Consider Using the N-Word Less," Grist, September 4, 2007. Reproduced by permission. http://www.grist.org.

chaos and pain to our world. The networks and newspapers have begun running urgent stories almost daily: The Greenland ice sheet is vanishing! Sea levels are rising! Wildfires are out of control! Hurricanes are getting bigger!

There is precious little popular discussion of banning the abusive practices that directly create violent climate change.

But what's the solution? Most media sidebars and web links quickly send us to that peppy and bright list we all know so well, one vaguely reminiscent of *Better Homes and Gardens*: "10 Things *You* Can Do to Save the Planet." Standard steps include: change three light bulbs. Consider a hybrid car for your next purchase. Tell the kids to turn out the lights. Even during the recent [2007] Al Gore-inspired Live Earth concerts, the phrase "planetary emergency" was followed by "wear more clothes indoors in winter" and "download your music at home to save on the shipping fuel for CDs."

Nice little gestures all, but are you kidding me? Does anyone think this is the answer?

Laws, Not Voluntary Actions

Imagine if this had been the dominant response to racial segregation 50 years ago. Apartheid rules across much of our land and here are three things you can do: Take time, if possible, to feed three negroes who seek food at your lunch counter each month. Consider giving up your use of the N-word, or at least cut down. And avoid vacationing in states where National Guardsmen are needed to enroll blacks in public schools.

Obviously, there are times in history when moral, economic, and national-security wrongs are so huge that appeals for voluntary change are not only wildly insufficient but are themselves immoral as a dominant national response. By 1965 we had appropriately *banned* racial discrimination in housing, employment, voting, and other realms of national life. The majority of Americans understood this to be the only appropriate response to a colossal national injustice.

Global warming is a full-blown emergency and we have very little time to fix it.

Meanwhile, global warming represents an even greater source of potential human suffering, not just to us, but to all humans—and not just now, but for centuries to come. And yet there is precious little popular discussion of banning the abusive practices that directly create violent climate change. Like Jim Crow practices, we must by law phase out completely the manufacture of inefficient light bulbs and gas-guzzling cars, as a serious start to fighting this problem.

Next time Aunt Betty goes to buy bulbs at the CVS, there should *only* be climate-friendly fluorescents for sale. When she shops for her next car, there should *only* be 50-mpg models across the lot, the sort even Detroit admits it can readily build.

Of course, there are politicians and activists already out there passionately calling for dramatic statutory responses to global warming. But they are mostly drowned out by the "10 Things You Can Do" chorus. And it turns out the voluntary "green your lifestyle" mantra may in fact discourage even individual change. One British study found that people tend to respond in one of two ways when told simultaneously that global warming is a planetary emergency and that the solution is switching a few light bulbs: they conclude that a) the problem can't be that big if my few bulbs can fix it, so I won't worry about any of it; or b) I know the problem is huge and my little bulbs can't really make a difference, so why bother?

While I do believe we have a moral responsibility to do what we can as individuals, we just don't have enough time to win this battle one household at a time, street by painstaking street, from coast to coast.

The Actions That Really Matter

Here, finally, are the only facts that matter. First, global warming *is* a full-blown emergency and we have very little time to fix it. Second, ours is a nation of laws and if we want to change our nation—profoundly and in a hurry—we must change our laws. I'd rather have 100,000 Americans phoning their U.S. senators twice per week demanding a prompt phaseout of inefficient automobile engines and light bulbs than 1 million Americans willing to "eat their vegetables" and voluntarily fill up their driveway and houses with the right stuff.

The problem at hand is so huge it requires a response like our national mobilization to fight—and win—World War II. To move our nation off of fossil fuels, we need inspired Churchillian leadership and sweeping statutes a la the Big War or the civil-rights movement.

So frankly, I feel a twinge of nausea now each time I see that predictable "10 Things You Can Do" sidebar in a well-meaning magazine or newspaper article. In truth, the only list that actually matters is the one we should all be sending to Congress post haste, full of 10 muscular clean-energy statutes that would finally do what we say we want: rescue our life-giving Earth from climate catastrophe.

9

Laws Curbing Emissions Are Necessary and Can Encourage Profitability

Fred Krupp

Fred Krupp is the president of the Environmental Defense Fund.

The McCain-Lieberman Climate Stewardship Act, introduced in 2003 by Senators John McCain and Joseph Lieberman, is designed to cap carbon dioxide emissions at year-2000 levels by 2010. Achieving the bill's goals would require new technologies to decrease greenhouse gases, creating an emissions trading market to provide companies with financial initiatives to reduce their output. Such legislation, which would apply to numerous industries, would be successful because it would effectively reduce emissions while enabling industries to remain profitable.

I appreciate the opportunity to testify here today [January 8, 2003] on what Environmental Defense considers one of the most urgent environmental problems of our time—global climate change. I am very pleased, moreover, that the focus of the hearing is the impressive proposal offered by Senators [John] McCain and [Joseph] Lieberman (shared with Environmental Defense in draft form on December 20, [2002]) to

Fred Krupp, "The McCain-Lieberman Climate Change Proposal: The Importance of a Comprehensive 'Cap-and-Trade' Framework to Reduce Greenhouse Gas Emissions," Testimony given before the Committee on Commerce, Science and Transportation, U.S. Senate, January 8, 2003.

tackle that problem.[1] Finally, I am particularly grateful to this Committee for the previous hearings it has conducted to create a sound, well-balanced record of scientific understanding of global climate change.

Thanks to those hearings, I know that my testimony on the McCain-Lieberman legislation will be considered against a backdrop of increased understanding. First, there is strong scientific consensus that human activities contribute substantially to the buildup of heat-trapping greenhouse gases (GHG) in the atmosphere. Second, if GHG emissions continue to rise, the world will face increasingly devastating environmental disruptions affecting not only our most precious natural ecosystems but also, potentially, the world food supply and human health.

This state of affairs challenges our American values and our American ingenuity. Fortunately, I believe that, taken as a whole, the McCain-Lieberman bill is a serious and credible response. . . .

Climate Change and American Values

Our success in this endeavor will require responsible environmental stewardship—one of the bedrock values held by Americans.

The GHG emissions produced by the first automobile that rolled off the assembly line in Detroit are still in the atmosphere. Each new ton of greenhouse gases emitted today will reside in the atmosphere for decades. Over time, the resulting warming will change the climate—and the environment—in countless ways. Impacts could range from the die-off of coral reefs to the loss of vital fisheries to sharply increased cycles of storms and drought. Sea level rise could be so severe that the entire National Mall here in Washington would be flooded

1 The Climate Stewardship Act was defeated in the Senate in 2003, and a modified version was defeated in 2005. Yet another version was introduced in 2007, and had not yet been voted on as of late 2008.

regularly. That this could be the legacy of our own everyday actions is a notion that few Americans alive today would knowingly tolerate. America's commitment to caring for our natural heritage prompts us to demand that our national leaders take responsible actions to help curb global warming.

Responsible stewardship requires that we take the necessary steps to protect the climate from the harmful effects of GHG emissions. Because greenhouse gases build up incrementally in the atmosphere, stabilizing their *concentrations* will require very significant reductions in *emissions* over the next century. Moreover, most scientists agree that in order to avoid the kind of drastic environmental damage that most would consider unacceptable, substantial reductions in total GHG emissions must begin *now*. Highly respected analyses indicate that world leaders have a narrow time window in which to act. Failure to begin reducing total GHG emissions within the next decade (the period covered by the McCain-Lieberman bill) may foreclose the chance our children and grandchildren have to avert dangerous climate change in the future.

Climate Change and American Ingenuity

Throughout history, American ingenuity has enabled our nation to triumph over adversity. We need to unleash that same can-do spirit today to help curb global warming. The challenge arises from the fact that GHG emissions are the direct result of fundamental economic activities—like producing energy, food and clothing, transporting ourselves and our goods, using our lands and forests and even creating and sharing data. No matter how powerful our commitment to environmental protection is, unless we can ensure our continued economic prosperity, policies seeking to reduce GHG emissions likely will not succeed.

That's where Americans' ability to solve problems comes in. Achieving significant GHG reductions that the economy can afford will require inventiveness and entrepreneurship.

The good news is that climate change *is* a man-made problem, and thus can be addressed by human actions. Our nation's record of success in attaining high levels of environmental protection while enjoying continual economic growth suggests that curbing U.S. GHG emissions not only is eminently affordable, but also could bring about a host of benefits to the public. The best GHG policies will be those that set clear emissions reduction targets and explicitly allow businesses and individuals to seek out a broad mix of the strategies. Through experimentation and innovation, they will devise new technologies and invest in GHG emissions reductions that deliver the biggest environmental and social payoff at lowest cost. At the same time, it is critical that those policies be as close to all-encompassing as possible, so that energy producers, industrial manufacturers, farmers and landowners and other key economic actors have a chance to contribute their expertise to the search for the best ways to reduce GHG emissions.

Tightening the reduction levels and timetable now in the bill will only enhance our legacy to future generations.

This approach reflects more than just blind faith or naïve optimism. Anticipating the eventual need to comply with GHG requirements, many firms and landowners already are experimenting successfully with GHG reduction strategies. Several years ago, DuPont, a charter member of Environmental Defense's Partnership for Climate Action (PCA), announced its intention to cut its GHG emissions by 65% by 2010. In 2001, the company reached, and surpassed, that goal, nine years ahead of schedule. Since 1990, DuPont has succeeded in holding its energy use at 1990 levels. In 2000 alone, the program yielded a $325 million savings; overall the company attributes a $1.65 billion savings to its program.

In Washington State, the Pacific Northwest Direct Seed Association, representing 300 farmers owning 500,000 acres, has joined with Entergy, the power company, to promote direct seeding, a practice that enhances soil carbon sequestration and provides a host of other benefits such as improved soil productivity, reduced erosion and better wildlife habitat. In this partnership, Entergy will lease 30,000 tons of carbon offsets over a ten-year period from participating landowners. In addition to the carbon benefits to the atmosphere, the lands affected by the project will contribute less runoff to nearby waterways, helping to improve the habitat for critical steelhead and salmon runs.

Finally, perhaps the best-known example of can-do success in reducing GHG emissions is that of BP, the global petrochemical company. In 1998, the company launched a private initiative to reduce its GHG emissions 10% below 1990 levels by 2010. Last year, BP announced that it had achieved its target eight years ahead of schedule, and at no net cost to the business, all while achieving steady and robust economic growth.

These are not theoretical models, but real-life actions. In addition to BP, DuPont and Entergy, Environmental Defense has also been working with Alcan, Pechiney, Ontario Power Generation, Suncor and Shell in the Partnership for Climate Action (www.pca-online.org). Each of these firms has established a cap on GHG emissions voluntarily and is undertaking measures to limit emissions to the committed levels. Each company is succeeding in its efforts, while continuing to prosper.

McCain-Lieberman and Environmental Stewardship

Environmental Defense believes that the McCain-Lieberman bill embodies America's core commitment to responsible environmental stewardship. First, it would deliver the single most crucial response to the dangers of climate change—actual reductions in GHG emissions below current levels. The current policy debate on climate change features a host of potential approaches, including voluntary initiatives, technology subsidies and tax-like schemes such as cost safety-valves. None of these, however, would accomplish what this bill would do—guarantee actual reductions in GHG emissions. Again, to curb the unwanted effects of climate change means limiting the *concentrations* of greenhouse gases in the atmosphere. GHG concentrations can be limited *only* by reducing actual emissions. McCain-Lieberman would do just that—mandate the reduction of U.S. GHG emissions.

Second, the bill mandates GHG reductions below current levels by the middle of the next decade. Our best analysis suggests that this requirement could keep open the window of opportunity that policy-makers in the future must have if they are to achieve sufficient reductions for ultimate success in curbing climate change over the balance of the century.

Since GHG emissions build up in the atmosphere, every year of delay in reducing emissions is akin to playing another round of "global climate roulette." The ambitious use of emissions trading and flexibility will increase affordability and spur even greater and earlier GHG reductions than are required in the bill as currently drafted. Tightening the reduction levels and timetable now in the bill will only enhance our legacy to future generations. Again, because of the long-lived nature of greenhouse gases in the atmosphere, by achieving even greater reductions sooner, the bill would make it that much easier for future generations to achieve the reductions needed to solve the climate problem on a long-term basis.

McCain-Lieberman and American Ingenuity—and Economic Prosperity

By requiring GHG emissions reductions across virtually all sectors of the U.S. economy, the McCain-Lieberman bill taps the know-how and inventiveness of the broadest possible swath of economic players. It does so by integrating in a GHG emissions trading market virtually every major economic sector that can contribute to solving this problem, including transportation, agriculture and forestry.

Opponents of mandatory GHG reduction policies often claim that such policies would cost too much and stifle economic growth. They also question whether the kinds of innovations needed to achieve reductions can be found in the near term. By incorporating emissions trading as its centerpiece (along with a mandatory emissions cap), the McCain-Lieberman legislation emulates one of the most successful environmental programs in U.S. history—the federal acid rain program. Under the McCain-Lieberman approach, companies that achieve more GHG reductions than required can save their extra reductions to use against their own future emissions increases or can trade those reductions to other companies that are having trouble meeting their emissions limits.

Historically, releases of carbon dioxide from land-use activities have contributed substantially to increased concentrations of atmospheric greenhouse gases.

Consequently, companies will have a direct financial incentive and unlimited opportunity to make as many low-cost reductions as possible as soon as possible. That means that the lowest-cost reducers will be acting in a way that will result in overall compliance costs being lower. It also means innovative companies that achieve more reductions than required will be financially rewarded by the emissions trading market. The emissions trading framework provides flexibility for companies to change and grow while meeting their emissions requirements at the same time.

In 1990, Congress used a similar approach to achieve reductions in sulfur dioxide, a chief cause of acid rain. Sulfur dioxide emissions at U.S. power plants were reduced and capped through a program that allowed the plants to save or trade extra emissions reductions. As a result, the acid rain program has achieved more total reductions than required, at lower cost than predicted and through technological innovations not seen under previous air pollution programs. Meanwhile, the power sector has enjoyed steady economic growth. Emissions trading can also be a useful tool for reducing GHG emissions because their environmental effects are not local, but national and global. Thus, it is the quantity of reductions achieved, not their location, that determines the environmental success of the program.

Simply put, the acid rain emissions trading program has done what markets do best—drive down costs. The economic performance of the McCain-Lieberman emissions trading system can be expected to be even more robust than that of the acid rain emissions trading system. The latter covered only the power sector in the United States. The McCain-Lieberman market would embrace a vastly more numerous and more diverse set of economic actors. Standard economic theory suggests that their number and diversity would intensify the search for cost savings by the participants and would more richly reward that search by providing an enormous multiplicity of cost-effective reduction opportunities.

By creating a market, the McCain-Lieberman bill takes the challenge of cost head-on and meets it with the most powerful of cost-savings tools. It is in markets that Americans' relentless ingenuity, the engine of our nation's economy, has always thrived. . . .

The Importance of Forests and Farmland

While climate and energy policies are inextricably linked, climate policy demands more than just a re-tooling of the nation's energy, industrial and transportation sectors. The

McCain-Lieberman bill is pioneering a comprehensive and rational climate policy that encompasses the effects of land use as well.

The Earth's climate is warming as a result of increasing concentrations of atmospheric greenhouse gases released not just from energy and industrial sources but also through land-use activities. Most significantly, these activities include forest management and agricultural practices in both croplands and grasslands. As forests grow, they absorb vast amounts of carbon dioxide from the atmosphere through photosynthesis. This carbon is then sequestered in woods, leaves, roots and soils (hence the term "carbon sequestration"). When forests are harvested, burned, or cleared for agriculture, much of the carbon stored in plant matter and soils is emitted into the atmosphere as carbon dioxide, the primary greenhouse gas.

Agricultural activities also play an important role in the global carbon cycle as croplands and grasslands store large amounts of carbon. Practices such as conservation tillage, grassland restoration and use of cover crops enhance carbon storage in agricultural soils. In contrast, land clearing and plowing release carbon dioxide by exposing soils to air and sunlight.

Cost savings through emissions trading in no way would lessen the amount of total emissions reductions or their environmental benefit.

By sequestering carbon, forests and agricultural lands can act as a carbon "sink." The capacity of soils and biomass to remove carbon from the atmosphere depends upon location, soil type, vegetation type, climate, human or natural disturbances, and other factors.

Historically, releases of carbon dioxide from land-use activities have contributed substantially to increased concentrations of atmospheric greenhouse gases. Prior to the surge in human activities, primarily the burning of fossil fuels, atmospheric concentrations of CO_2 were around 280 parts per million (ppm). Today, CO_2 concentrations are approximately 378 ppm. . . .

In view of this, Environmental Defense believes that Senators McCain and Lieberman made the correct fundamental choice in allowing farmers and landowners to opt to participate in the GHG reduction market. Within the framework of a cap-and-trade system, investments in the land-use sector can provide a critical mass of cost-effective, high-yield emission reduction opportunities. Thus, emissions reductions made through carbon sequestration have the potential to play a valuable role in a broad ensemble of tools to combat climate change.

In our view, both the environmental performance and the economic performance of a GHG reduction market demand that in the search for carbon sequestration and GHG reduction opportunities, farmers and landowners be allowed to act on a level playing field with other emissions sources. To ensure such a level playing field, land-use-generated GHG "credits" must be rigorously proven to represent real, surplus and durable reductions or increments of sequestration to the same degree that surplus GHG emissions allowances or allotments do. This stricture, far more than the imposition of quantitative limits on the use of land-use-generated credits, will be key to ensuring the environmental integrity of a GHG trading system that encompasses sequestration and other land-related crediting.

McCain-Lieberman and Regulatory Innovation

Thanks to its use of the cap-and-trade framework, the McCain-Lieberman bill, like the federal acid rain program, introduces a noteworthy regulatory innovation. Under the bill, it would be businesses and landowners, not governmental officials or regulators, who would be making the pivotal choice in determining the best means of compliance. The bill would establish that GHG sources are legally accountable for achieving a specified level of emissions reductions and to continually monitor and report their actual emissions. The regulators' only job would be to ensure that each source meets its monitoring and reporting requirements and that its actual annual emissions equal its allotment of allowable emissions.

How sources reduce their GHG emissions would be left completely to the discretion of their operators. As a result, it would be up to them to adapt to the continually changing economic and technical circumstances while still meeting their emissions cap. The burden and the opportunity of lowering costs would be placed squarely on the firms. In place of regulatory variances and other cost-relieving methods that entail compromise of standards and forego actual emissions reductions, firms under a cap-and-trade system must turn to emissions banking and trading for cost control. Because of the built-in cap-based structure of the bill, cost savings through emissions trading in no way would lessen the amount of total emissions reductions or their environmental benefit.

10

Policies Curbing Emissions Are Unnecessary and Hinder Profitability

James M. Inhofe

James M. Inhofe, a Republican from Oklahoma, became a U.S. Senator in 1994. He is the former chairman of the Senate Committee on Environment and Public Works.

Climate change has been a fact of life for centuries, and the relatively recent concern over rising temperatures is being exaggerated by environmental alarmists. Scientists disagree whether climate change is even happening, much less to what extent the temperature might fluctuate in the future. Initiatives to curb greenhouse gas emissions—most notably the Kyoto Protocol—are based on suspect science and will place undue financial pressure on the United States to bring its emissions levels to what are considered acceptable by Kyoto. In addition, Kyoto and other proposals have not demonstrated that they would have a significant effect on curbing climate change.

The climate is constantly changing, and has done so throughout history. The challenge is to understand the natural changes in the climate and whether humans are contributing significantly to those changes. The larger challenge is to separate the politics from the discussion of the science, in order to better understand the state of knowledge of climate change science.

James M. Inhofe, "The Facts and Science of Climate Change," U.S. Senate Committee on Environment and Public Works, 2004. http://epw.senate.gov/repwhitepapers/ClimateChangeWebuse.pdf.

Today, even saying there is scientific disagreement over global warming is itself controversial. But anyone who pays even cursory attention to the issue understands that scientists vigorously disagree over whether human activities are responsible for global warming, or whether those activities will precipitate apocalyptic natural disasters.

It is extremely important for the future of this country that the facts and the science get a fair hearing. Without proper knowledge and understanding, alarmists will scare the country into enacting their ultimate goal: making energy suppression, in the form of harmful mandatory restrictions on carbon dioxide and other greenhouse emissions, the official policy of the United States.

Such a policy would induce serious economic harm, especially for low-income and minority populations. Energy suppression, as official government and nonpartisan private analyses have amply confirmed, means higher prices for food, medical care, and electricity, as well as massive job losses and drastic reductions in gross domestic product, all the while providing virtually no environmental benefit. In other words: a raw deal for the American people.

Unfortunately, much of the debate over global warming is predicated on fear, rather than science. Global warming alarmists see a future plagued by catastrophic flooding, war, terrorism, economic dislocations, droughts, crop failures, mosquitoborne diseases, and harsh weather all caused by manmade greenhouse gas emissions. . . .

The Kyoto Protocol

The issue of global warming has garnered significant international attention through the Kyoto Protocol, a treaty which requires signatories to reduce their greenhouse gas emissions by considerable amounts below 1990 levels. [The Kyoto Protocol operates on a "cap-and-trade" system that imposes national caps on developed countries' emissions.]

The [Bill] Clinton Administration, led by former Vice President Al Gore, signed the Kyoto Protocol on November 12, 1998, but never submitted it to the Senate for ratification.

The treaty explicitly acknowledges as true that manmade emissions, principally from the use of fossil fuels, are causing global temperatures to rise, eventually to catastrophic levels. Kyoto enthusiasts believe that if we dramatically cut back, or even eliminate, fossil fuels, the climate system will respond by sending global temperatures back to "normal" levels.

In 1997, the Senate sent a powerful signal that Kyoto was unacceptable. By a vote of 95 to 0, the Senate passed the Byrd/Hagel resolution, which stated that the Senate would not ratify Kyoto if it were to cause substantial economic harm and if developing countries were not required to participate on the same timetable.

Kyoto, and Kyoto-like policies, would cause the greatest harm to the poorest among us.

Some of the Problems with Kyoto

The treaty would have required the U.S. to reduce its emissions 31% below the level otherwise predicted for 2010. Put another way, the U.S. would have had to cut 552 million metric tons of CO_2 per year by 2008–2012. As the Business Roundtable pointed out, that target is "the equivalent of having to eliminate all current emissions from either the U.S. transportation sector, or the utilities sector (residential and commercial sources), or industry."

The most widely cited and most definitive economic analysis of Kyoto came from Wharton Econometric Forecasting Associates, or WEFA, (a private consulting company founded by professors from the University of Pennsylvania's Wharton Business School). According to WEFA economists, Kyoto would cost 2.4 million U.S. jobs and reduce GDP by 3.2%, or about $300 billion annually, an amount greater than the total expenditure on primary and secondary education.

Because of Kyoto, American consumers would face higher food, medical, and housing costs: for food, an increase of 11%; medicine, an increase of 14%; and housing, an increase of 7%. At the same time an average household of four would see its real income drop by $2,700 in 2010, and each year thereafter.

Under Kyoto, energy and electricity prices would nearly double, and gasoline prices would go up an additional 65 cents per gallon.

Some in the environmental community have dismissed the WEFA report as a tainted product of "industry"; however, a 1998 analysis by the Clinton Energy Information Administration, the statistical arm of the Department of Energy, largely confirmed WEFA's analysis.

Despite these facts, radical groups such as Greenpeace blindly assert that Kyoto "will not impose significant costs" and "will not be an economic burden."

Who Will Be Harmed by Kyoto?

Among the many questions this provokes, one might ask: Won't be a burden on whom, exactly? Greenpeace doesn't elaborate, but according to a recent study by the Center for Energy and Economic Development ["Refusing to Repeat Past Mistakes," 2000], sponsored by the National Black Chamber of Commerce and the United States Hispanic Chamber of Commerce, if the U.S. ratifies Kyoto, or passes domestic climate policies effectively implementing the treaty, the result would "disproportionately harm America's minority communities, and place the economic advancement of millions of U.S. Blacks and Hispanics at risk."

Among the study's key findings: Kyoto will cost 511,000 jobs held by Hispanic workers and 864,000 jobs held by Black workers; poverty rates for minority families will increase dramatically; and, because Kyoto will bring about higher energy prices, many minority businesses will be lost.

It is interesting to note that the environmental left purports to advocate policies based on their alleged good for humanity, especially for the most vulnerable. Kyoto is no exception. Yet Kyoto, and Kyoto-like policies, would cause the greatest harm to the poorest among us.

Environmental alarmists, as an article of faith, peddle the notion that climate change is, as Greenpeace put it, "the biggest environmental threat facing developing countries." For one, such thinking runs contrary to the public declaration of the 2002 World Summit on Sustainable Development—a program sponsored by the United Nations—which found that *poverty* is the number one threat facing developing countries.

Dr. John Christy, director of the Earth System Science Center at the University of Alabama, Huntsville, passionately reiterated that point in a May 22 [2003] letter to House Resources Committee Chairman Richard Pombo (R. Calif.). As an addendum to his testimony during the committee's hearing on the Kyoto Protocol, Christy, an Alabama state climatologist, wrote eloquently about his service as a missionary in Africa.

For Christy, "poverty is the worst polluter," and as he noted, bringing modern, inexpensive electricity to developing countries would raise living standards and lead to a cleaner environment. Kyoto, he said, would be counterproductive, for Kyoto would divert precious resources away from helping those truly in need to a problem that doesn't exist, and a solution that would have no environmental benefit.

Some senators have introduced Kyoto-like legislation that would hurt low-income and minority populations. Last year, Tom Mullen, president of Cleveland Catholic Charities, testified against S. 556, the Clean Power Act, which would impose onerous, unrealistic restrictions, including a Kyoto-like cap on carbon dioxide emissions, on electric utilities. He noted that this regime would mean higher electricity prices for the poorest citizens of Cleveland.

For those on fixed incomes, as Mr. Mullen pointed out, higher electricity prices present a choice between eating and staying warm in winter or cool in summer. As Mr. Mullen said, "The overall impact on the economy in Northeast Ohio would be overwhelming, and the needs that we address at Catholic Charities in Ohio with the elderly and poor would be well beyond our capacity and that of our current partners in government and the private sector."

Kyoto and Developing Countries

In addition to its negative economic impacts, Kyoto still does not satisfy Byrd/Hagel's concerns about developing countries. Though such countries as China, India, Brazil, South Korea, and Mexico are signatories to Kyoto, they are not required to reduce their emissions, even though they emit nearly 30 percent of the world's greenhouse gases. And within a generation they will be the world's largest emitters of carbon, methane and other such greenhouse gases.

Despite the fact that neither of Byrd/Hagel's conditions has been met, environmentalists have bitterly criticized President [George W.] Bush for abandoning Kyoto. But one wonders: why don't they assail the 95 senators, both Democrats and Republicans, who, according to Byrd/Hagel, oppose Kyoto as it stands today, and who would, presumably, oppose ratification if the treaty came up on the Senate floor? Neither do they assail former President Clinton, or former Vice President Gore, who signed the treaty but never submitted it to the Senate for ratification.

Remember, Byrd/Hagel said the Senate would not ratify Kyoto if it caused substantial economic harm and if developing countries were not required to participate on the same timetable. So, if the Bryd/Hagel conditions are ever satisfied, should the United States ratify Kyoto?

Kyoto and the Environment

Answering that question depends on several factors, including whether Kyoto would provide significant, needed environmental benefits.

First, we should ask what Kyoto is designed to accomplish. According to the U.N.'s Intergovernmental Panel on Climate Change [IPCC], Kyoto will achieve "stabilization of greenhouse gas concentrations in the atmosphere at a level that would prevent dangerous anthropogenic interference with the climate system."

Kyoto . . . will have virtually no impact on global temperatures.

What does this statement mean? The IPCC offers no elaboration and doesn't provide any scientific explanation about what that level would be. Why? The answer is simple: thus far no one has found a definitive scientific answer.

Dr. S. Fred Singer, an atmospheric scientist at the University of Virginia, who served as the first director of the U.S. Weather Satellite Service (which is now in the Department of Commerce) and more recently as a member and vice chairman of the National Advisory Committee on Oceans and Atmosphere (NACOA), said that "No one knows what constitutes a 'dangerous' concentration. There exists, as yet, no scientific basis for defining such a concentration, or even of knowing whether it is more or less than current levels of carbon dioxide."

One might pose the question: if we had the ability to set the global thermostat, what temperature would we pick? Would we set it colder or warmer than it is today? What would the optimal temperature be? The actual dawn of civilization occurred in a period climatologists call the "climatic optimum" when the mean surface temperature was 121 [degrees] Celsius warmer than today. Why not go 1 to 2 degrees Celsius higher? Or 1 to 2 degrees lower for that matter?

The Kyoto emissions reduction targets are arbitrary, lacking in any real scientific basis. Kyoto therefore will have virtually no impact on global temperatures. This is not merely an opinion, but the conclusion reached by the country's top climate scientists.

Climate alarmists see an opportunity here to tax the American people.

Dr. Tom Wigley, a senior scientist at the National Center for Atmospheric Research, found that if the Kyoto Protocol were fully implemented by all signatories, it would reduce temperatures by a mere 0.07 degrees Celsius by 2050, and 0.13 degrees Celsius by 2100. What does this mean? Such an amount is so small that ground-based thermometers cannot reliably measure it.

Dr. Richard Lindzen, an MIT [Massachusetts Institute of Technology] scientist and member of the National Academy of Sciences, who has specialized in climate issues for over 30 years, told the Committee on Environment and Public Works on May 2, 2001 that there is a "definitive disconnect between Kyoto and science. Should a catastrophic scenario prove correct, Kyoto will not prevent it."

Similarly, Dr. James Hansen of NASA [National Aeronautics and Space Administration], considered the father of global warming theory, said that Kyoto Protocol "will have little effect" on global temperature in the 21st century. In a rather stunning followup, Hansen said it would take *30 Kyotos* to reduce warming to an acceptable level. If one Kyoto devastates the American economy, what would 30 do?...

The Next Steps

It is mystifying that some people blithely assert that the science of global warming is settled—that fossil fuel emissions are the principal, driving cause of global warming.

In a recent letter concerning the next EPA [Environmental Protection Agency] administrator, two senators wrote that "the pressing problem of global warming" is now an "established scientific fact," and demanded that the new administrator commit to addressing it.

With all due respect, this statement is baseless, for several reasons. As outlined in detail above, the evidence is overwhelmingly in favor of those who don't see global warming posing grave harm to the planet and who don't think human beings have significant influence on the climate system.

Climate alarmists see an opportunity here to tax the American people. Consider a July 11 [2003] op-ed by J.W. Anderson in the *Washington Post*. In it, Anderson, a former editorial writer for the *Post*, and now a journalist in residence with Resources for the Future, concedes that climate science still confronts uncertainties, then argues for a fuel tax to prepare for a potentially catastrophic future. Such a course of action fits a particular ideological agenda, yet is entirely unwarranted.

Hopefully, Congress will reject prophets of doom who peddle propaganda masquerading as science in the name of saving the planet from catastrophic disaster. We must put stock in scientists who rely on the best, most objective scientific data and reject fear as a motivating basis for making public policy decisions. Alarmists are attempting to enact an agenda of energy suppression that is inconsistent with American values of freedom, prosperity, and environmental progress.

11

Air Travel Contributes to Climate Change

Gregory M. Lamb

Gregory M. Lamb is a staff writer for the Christian Science Monitor.

As air travel in the late twentieth and early twenty-first century has become increasingly affordable, the number of people relying on planes for both business and leisure travel has increased. Accordingly, the number of planes flying, and the amount of fuel that they burn, has increased as well. Environmentalists, politicians, and citizens are concerned that as the number of planes in use continues to grow, the amount of CO_2 jets release will grow rapidly. Compounding this problem is the fact that no viable alternative to jet fuel has been developed.

Just a few decades from now, people may look back at the early 21st century with both fondness and horror as the Era of the Cheap Airline Flight. They may wax nostalgic for the days when visiting distant relatives and taking vacations in exotic locales were easily affordable for the masses. But they also may be alarmed at how long it took the world to realize the havoc that unfettered air travel was wreaking on the world's climate.

At least one travel industry official predicts that in 30 years, long-distance flying will be undertaken only by the wealthy as ticket prices rise dramatically—and the number of

Gregory M. Lamb, "Flying the Cleanly Skies?" *The Christian Science Monitor*, February 12, 2007. Reproduced by permission from Christian Science Monitor, (www.cs monitor.com).

flights shrinks proportionately—to curb the emissions of greenhouse gases created by air travel.

A new air traffic management system could yield a 12 to 15 percent improvement in environmental performance.

Jet engines burn kerosene, which gives off carbon dioxide (CO_2), a leading cause of global warming. Airline flights today make up less than 3 percent of man-made CO_2 emissions, though they also spew nitrogen oxide, sulfur dioxide, soot, and water vapor that may double their total warming effect on the climate.

Now two factors are conspiring to make airline travel a hot topic in the global-warming debate: If current trends continue, the number of airline tickets sold per year will double to more than 9 billion by 2025, according to a new study by the Airports Council International. At the same time, exports see no viable jet-fuel alternative to kerosene. While some modest fuel-conservation measures still can be taken, more and more people are concluding that fewer flights may be the only way to cut airline emissions significantly.

The Britain Example

In Britain, a prosperous island country that makes heavy use of air travel, CO_2 emissions from flights will surpass those from automobile trips in the next six to eight years, says Alice Bows, a senior research fellow at the Tyndall Centre for Climate Change Research at the University of Manchester.

Four years ago, the British government pledged to cut greenhouse-gas emissions by 60 percent by midcentury. As the difficulty in achieving that goal has become more evident, air travel has become the whipping boy for environmentalists. Prime Minister Tony Blair was criticized for flying to Miami for a Christmas holiday, and Prince Charles was viewed as a hypocrite for boarding a jet to Philadelphia to accept an environmental award. Last summer, the Bishop of London, Richard Chartres, called taking a vacation by airline "a symptom of sin" in which "people ignore the consequences of their actions." The bishop vowed he would not board an airplane in 2007.

Asking the British people to cut down on air travel is impractical, Mr. Blair says. But the government has just upped a tax on airline flights from £10 to £40 ($19 to $76), depending on the length of the flight, in the name of reducing air travel and CO_2 emissions.

Innovations and Ideas

For years, airline companies have worked to increase fuel efficiency (and coincidentally reduce CO_2 emissions) to counter the skyrocketing price of kerosene. New aircraft, such as Boeing's 787 Dreamliner due out in the summer of 2008, will be made of lighter composite materials and employ other fuel-saving measures. But these improvements won't be nearly enough to offset the predicted increase in demand for air travel (including air freight).

Other fuel-saving suggestions include pulling planes from the gate to the runway with their engines only idling, reducing the fuel used to taxi into position for takeoff.

Modernized air-traffic control systems could reduce the number of planes circling airports waiting to land or take off, says John Meenan, executive vice president of the Air Transport Association of America, which represents the nation's airlines. Commercial airliners today follow ground beacons to their destinations that result in indirect and inefficient zigzag routes, Mr. Meenan says. A new air traffic management system could yield a 12 to 15 percent improvement in environmental performance.

"It's a matter of making the investment to make that happen," he says.

In the long term, biofuels, possibly ethanol made from switch grass or biowaste, could provide an alternative. But no one knows when that could happen. "One of the realities we're dealing with in aviation is that there are no alternatives" to CO_2-emitting kerosene fuels, Meenan says.

The European Union has proposed incorporating aviation into its carbon-emissions trading plan by 2011, a so-called "cap and trade" scheme. That would allow airlines to "buy" the right to emit carbon from other industries, such as power generation, which could sell carbon credits if they reduced their emissions below their cap.

Other Effects of Flying Less

People aren't going to give up airline travel easily. For long-distance travel, there's really no practical replacement. "We think the free movement of people and goods is a pretty fundamental right," says Graham Lancaster, a spokesman for Britain's Federation of Tour Operators.

The effect of a drastic reduction of airline flights on the world economy would be significant. Aviation drives about 9 percent of world GDP, Meenan says.

"The countries that would be hit hardest would be developing countries, because they're more dependent on tourism," says Justin Francis, CEO of responsibletravel.com, an online travel agency specializing in ecotourism based in Brighton, England. In half of the developing countries, tourism is one of the top three industries, he says.

"My view is that we must fly less," Mr. Francis says, adding that the ecoconscious might decide to take only one big vacation flight each year and take shorter nonflying vacations the rest of the year. Hopping around Europe every few weeks on the low-cost airlines that have sprung up in recent years would have to end, he says.

"The world is coming to realize the biggest threat we face is carbon emissions," Francis says. "Governments are under pressure to take action. One of the places they will look is the airline industry because it is such a rapidly growing source of emissions."

12

The Benefits of Air Travel Outweigh the Modest Impact on the Climate

Kendra Okonski

Kendra Okonski is the sustainable development director for the International Policy Network.

While politicians assert that air travel causes harm to the environment in the form of increased greenhouse gas emissions, the advantages of deregulated, cheap air travel go beyond enabling people to travel to previously unreachable locations; it benefits businesses and allows an increased amount of goods to be imported into countries. In addition, some of the most-referenced science claiming that air travel affects climate change is speculative, and long-term projections are inherently unreliable. Proposed taxes on air fares and jet fuel are likely to have unintended negative consequences. Finally, the amount of greenhouse gas emitted by jet travel is miniscule compared to the total amount of man-made emissions released into the atmosphere by developing countries and should not be singled out as a significant problem.

Vapour trails across the autumn sky have become the equivalent of the fortune-teller's tea leaves, spelling ecological doom. It's the one thing that David Cameron [British politician and Conservative Party leader since 2007] and David Miliband [British politician and secretary of state for foreign

Kendra Okonski, "Fear of Flying: Why Green Alarmists Are Wrong," *The Spectator*, November 2, 2006. Reproduced by permission of The Spectator.

and commonwealth affairs since 2007] seem to agree upon: cheap air travel will inundate the Earth's atmosphere with dangerous greenhouse gases unless it is curtailed by punitive taxes. The Stern report on the economic consequences of climate change provides all the justification either of them needs to propose policies ranging from adding VAT [value-added tax] to air fares and taxing aviation fuel, to forcing airlines into the EU [European Union] Emissions Trading Scheme, and even abolishing duty-free in-flight purchases.

If the benefits in terms of reduced probability of climate catastrophe are minuscule, what about the costs of the various proposals?

So just how guilty should we feel about last week's bargain half-term break? Should we cancel that trip abroad to celebrate Dad's birthday, and resist those 95p [pence] fare offers to soak up the winter sun? Until recently most people didn't have these options because air fares were prohibitively expensive. But in the past decade deregulation and competition have enabled more people to fly more frequently for business and leisure. Imported food and other air-lifted goods have become more affordable. Improvements in efficiency and competition have benefited consumers and producers at home and abroad.

Speculative Science

But green alarmists say this travel and commerce is irresponsible and unnecessary, and that aviation emissions contribute disproportionately to environmental damage because they are emitted at high altitude. Yet according to a report on aviation emissions from the Intergovernmental Panel on Climate Change (IPCC)—often referred to as the authoritative consensus of thousands of scientists—the science surrounding this topic is 'inevitably speculative': long-term projections about air traffic demand, fleet fuel burned and fleet emissions are 'unreliable—sometimes astoundingly so'. Campaigners invoke the IPCC's authority at every other opportunity, yet seem conveniently to have ignored this particular report.

Alarmists warn that between 1990 and 2050 Britain's aviation emissions will increase between four and ten times. But how important is this? No matter what their growth, our aviation emissions (currently about 5 per cent of all British emissions) will pale in comparison with increased emissions elsewhere. To put things in perspective, the increase in emissions from China every year is approximately equal to all of Britain's current annual emissions—which represent only about 2 per cent of the global total.

Where aviation and emissions are concerned, we should be very wary of politicians who brandish moralistic arguments to justify taxes which will ultimately yield few gains to us, or to the environment.

Where Taxes and Proposals Fail

This makes the government's commitment to reducing Britain's overall emissions by 60 per cent by 2050 look rather puny, because by that stage this will mean reducing global emissions by only perhaps half a per cent. And it makes reductions in aviation emissions look frankly pointless. Even if we stopped flying altogether, the reduction would amount to no more than a small fraction of 1 per cent of global emissions by 2050—assuming that aviation grows at the upper end of the predicted range and that jets largely fail to become more efficient. The tiny reduction that might result from any of the proposed punitive taxes is unlikely to have any noticeable effect on the world's climate. The measure of any policy should be whether its benefits outweigh its costs: if the benefits in terms of reduced probability of climate catastrophe are minuscule, what about the costs of the various proposals?

A tax on air fares might well achieve its objective of reducing air travel. But it would also reduce the profit margins of low-cost carriers, benefiting higher-cost airlines, which have—unsurprisingly—been far from critical of this proposal. Yet just because people are not travelling by air doesn't mean they are not travelling. Another touted advantage of taxing air fares is that Britain's tourism industry would benefit—if Britons who stay at home spend more than the foreigners who decide not to come. It means more use of other forms of transport, especially cars, but do we really want to increase the traffic on Britain's congested roads?

This would also be a snobs' tax, falling disproportionately on lower- and middle-income travellers. A 2004 Civil Aviation Authority passenger survey showed that 25 per cent of leisure travellers at Britain's major airports were 'lower income', with much of the remainder 'middle income'.

Cheap air travel also benefits business. Before easyJet and Ryanair, a short-haul trip departing on Monday and returning on Wednesday cost hundreds of pounds. Low-cost carriers have enabled businesses to cut costs; benefits are passed to consumers and shareholders through cheaper products and bigger dividends. Additional taxes would force low-cost carriers to eliminate some routes, causing a partial return to the bad old days of expensive mid-week flights—with negative consequences all round.

The next proposal is to tax jet fuel. This appears equitable at first, since jet fuel is currently untaxed, whereas fuel for road vehicles is notoriously heavily taxed. But its effects are more complex. Carriers flying to nearby non-EU countries such as Norway, Morocco and Tunisia could fill up on cheap, untaxed fuel, so the relative price of flights to those places would fall. Meanwhile, long-haul carriers would carry heavier fuel loads into the EU, and there would be a bias also towards carriers with refuelling hubs outside the EU. Perversely, these two effects could produce greater overall emissions.

Finally, some pundits say airlines should participate in the EU Emissions Trading Scheme (ETS). In fact, some older European carriers, both private and state-operated, have lobbied for mandatory participation—because again this would confer a competitive advantage: all airlines would receive ETS emissions permits based on their emissions in a given reference period, benefiting established carriers over younger competitors which may not have existed or were much smaller during the reference period.

Beyond the European Union

More important than these nuances is the overwhelming fact that greenhouse gas reductions by the EU will be swamped by future emissions from rapidly growing poorer countries—both from industry and aviation. The aspiring masses in those countries will undoubtedly choose to fly more, so their aviation emissions are likely to increase more rapidly than those of the EU. Aviation is growing fastest in Eastern Europe, the Middle East, Asia Pacific and Africa. Polish plumbers and their kin are becoming big customers of Europe's low-cost carriers: flights between Eastern European countries grew by 12 per cent in the past year.

But for now, these arguments can barely be heard. The loudest voices are those of the hardcore alarmists, with their 'moral' urge to compel us to consume less and fly less. [American writer] H.L. Mencken observed astutely that, 'The whole aim of practical politics is to keep the populace alarmed (and hence clamorous to be led to safety) by menacing it with an endless series of hobgoblins, all of them imaginary.' Where aviation and emissions are concerned, we should be very wary of politicians who brandish moralistic arguments to justify taxes which will ultimately yield few gains to us, or to the environment.

13

Green Consumerism Won't Benefit the Environment

Monica Hesse

Monica Hesse is a staff writer for the Washington Post.

As consumers have become more aware of climate change and its wide-ranging effects, so-called "green" products are becoming more popular and plentiful. From organic produce at local grocery stores to hybrid luxury cars to jewelry made from recycled materials, it is easier than ever to buy products that claim to benefit the environment. Just because such items are readily available, however, does not mean that purchasing them will actually help halt climate change. Buying new products without responsibly disposing of older ones—either through donation, recycling, or reuse—just adds to the problem of overconsumption, and can give consumers the false impression that it is possible to buy their way out of a climate crisis.

Congregation of the Church of the Holy Organic, let us buy.

Let us buy Anna Sova Luxury Organics Turkish towels, 900 grams per square meter, $58 apiece. Let us buy the eco-friendly 600-thread-count bed sheets, milled in Switzerland with U.S. cotton, $570 for queen-size.

Let us purge our closets of those sinful synthetics, purify ourselves in the flame of the soy candle at the altar of the immaculate Earth Weave rug, and let us *buy*, buy, buy until we are whipped into a beatific froth of free-range fulfillment.

Monica Hesse, "Greed in the Name of Green," *The Washington Post*, March 5, 2008. Reprinted with permission.

And let us never consider the other organic option—*not* buying—because the new green *consumer* wants to consume, to be more celadon than emerald, in the right color family but muted, without all the hand-me-down baby clothes and out-of-date carpet.

Consuming until you're squeaky green. It feels so good. It looks so good. It feels so good to look so good.

The New Green Consumer

There was a time, and it was pre-Al Gore, when buying organic meant eggs and tomatoes, Whole Foods and farmer's markets. But in the past two years, the word has seeped out of the supermarket and into the home store, into the vacation industry, into the Wal-Mart. Almost three-quarters of the U.S. population buys organic products at least occasionally; between 2005 and 2006 the sale of organic non-food items increased 26 percent, from $744 million to $938 million, according to the Organic Trade Association.

Green is the new black, carbon is the new kryptonite, blah blah blah. The privileged eco-friendly American realized long ago that SUVs were Death Stars; now we see that our gas-only Lexus is one, too. Best replace it with a 2008 LS 600 *hybrid* for $104,000 (it actually gets fewer miles per gallon than some traditional makes, but, see, it is a hybrid). Accessorize the interior with an organic Sherpa car seat cover for only $119.99.

Consuming until you're squeaky green. It feels so good. It looks so good. It feels so good to look so good, which is why conspicuousness is key.

These countertops are pressed paper.

Have I shown you my recycled platinum engagement ring?

In the past two weeks, our inbox has runneth over with giddily organic products: There's the 100 percent Organic Solana Swaddle Wrap, designed to replace baby blankets we did not even know were evil. There's the Valentine's pitch, "Forget Red—The color of love this season is Green!" It is advertising a water filter. There are the all-natural wasabi-covered goji berries, $30 for a snack six-pack, representing "a rare feat for wasabi."

There is the rebirth of *Organic Style* magazine, now only online but still as fashionable as ever, with a shopping section devoted to organic jewelry, organic pet bedding, organic garden decor, which apparently means more than "flowers" and "dirt."

When renowned environmentalist Paul Hawken is asked to comment on the new green consumer, he says, dryly, "The phrase itself is an oxymoron."

Oh ho?

"The good thing is people are waking up to the fact that we have a real [environmental] issue," says Hawken, who co-founded Smith & Hawken but left in 1992, before the $8,000 lawn became de rigueur. "But many of them are coming to the issue from being consumers. They buy a lot. They drive a lot."

They subscribe, in other words, to a destiny laid out by economist Victor Lebow, writing in 1955: "Our enormously productive economy demands that we make consumption our way of life, that we convert the buying and use of goods into rituals, that we seek our spiritual satisfaction ... in consumption. . . . We need things consumed, burned up, replaced and discarded at an ever-accelerating rate."

The Fallacies of Buying "Green"

The culture of obsolescence has become so deeply ingrained that it's practically reflexive. Holey sweaters get pitched, not mended. Laptops and cellphones get slimmer and shinier and smaller. We trade up every six months, and to make up for that, we buy and buy and hope we're buying the right *other* things, though sometimes we're not sure: When the Hartman

Group, a market research firm, asked a group of devout green consumers what the USDA "organic" seal meant when placed on a product, 43 percent did not know. (The seal means that the product is at least 95 percent organic—no pesticides, no synthetic hormones, no sewage sludge, no irradiation, no cloning.)

Which is why, when wannabe environmentalists try to change purchasing habits without also altering their consumer mind-set, something gets lost in translation.

The greenest products are the ones you don't buy.

Polyester = bad. Solution? Throw out the old wardrobe and replace with natural fibers!

Linoleum = bad. Solution? Rip up the old floor and replace with cork!

Out with the old, in with the green.

It's done with the best of intentions, but all that replacing is problematic. That "bad" vinyl flooring? It was probably less destructive in your kitchens than in a landfill (unless, of course, it was a health hazard). Ditto for the older, but still wearable, clothes.

And that's not even getting into the carbon footprint left by a nice duvet's 5,000-mile flight from Switzerland. (Oh, all right: a one-way ticket from Zurich to Washington produces about 1,500 pounds of carbon dioxide.)

Really going green, Hawken says, "means having less. It *does* mean less. Everyone is saying, 'You don't have to change your lifestyle.' Well, yes, actually, you *do*."

But, but, but—buying green feels so *guilt less*, akin to the mentality that results in eating 14 of Whole Foods' two-bite cupcakes. Their first ingredient is cane sugar, but in a land of high-fructose panic, that's practically a health food, right? Have another.

"There's a certain thrill that you get to go out and replace everything," says Leslie Garrett, author of "The Virtuous Consumer," a green shopping guide. "New bamboo T-shirts, new hemp curtains."

Garrett describes the conflicting feelings she and her husband experienced when trying to decide whether to toss an old living room sofa: "Our dog had chewed on it—there were only so many positions we could put it in" without the teeth marks showing. But it still fulfilled its basic role as a sofa: "We could still sit on it without falling through."

They could still make do. They could still, in this recession-wary economy, where everyone tries to cut back, subscribe to the crazy notion that conservation was about . . . conserving. Says Garrett, "The greenest products are the ones you don't buy."

An Eco-Friendly Compromise

There are exceptions. "Certain environmental issues trump other issues," Garrett says. "Preserving fossil fuels is more critical than landfill issues." If your furnace or fridge is functioning but inefficient, you can replace it guilt-free.

Ultimately, Garrett and her husband did buy a new sofa (from Ikea—Garrett appreciated the company's ban on carcinogens). But they made the purchase only after finding another home for their old couch—a college student on Craigslist was happy to take it off their hands.

The sofa example is what Josh Dorfman, host of the Seattle radio show "The Lazy Environmentalist," considers to be a best-case scenario for the modern consumer. "Buying stuff is intrinsically wrapped up in our identities," Dorfman says. "You can't change that behavior. It's better to say, 'You're a crazy shopaholic. You're not going to stop being a crazy shopaholic. But if you're going to buy 50 pairs of jeans, buy them from this better place.'"

Then again, his show is called "The Lazy Environmentalist."

Chip Giller, editor of enviro-blog Grist.org, has a less fatalistic view. He loves that Wal-Mart has developed an organic line. He applauds the efforts of the green consumer. "Two years ago, who would have thought we'd be in a place where terms like locavore [a person who eats only locally grown or raised foods] and carbon footprint were household terms?" he says, viewing green consumption as a "gateway" to get more people involved in environmental issues. The important thing is for people to keep walking through the gate, toward the land of reduced air travel, energy-efficient homes and much less stuff: "We're not going to buy our way out of this."

Congregation of the Church of the Holy Organic, let us scrub our sins away with Seventh Generation cleaning products. Let us go ahead and bite into the locally grown apple, and let us replace our incandescent light bulbs with those dreadfully expensive fluorescents.

But yea, though we walk through the valley of the luxury organic, let us purchase no imported Sherpa car seat covers. Let us use the old one, even though it is ugly, because our toddler will spill Pom juice on the organic one just as quickly as on the hand-me-down.

Amen.

Organizations to Contact

The editors have compiled the following list of organizations concerned with the issues debated in this book. The descriptions are derived from materials provided by the organizations. All have publications or information available for interested readers. The list was compiled on the date of publication of the present volume; the information provided here may change. Be aware that many organizations take several weeks or longer to respond to inquiries, so allow as much time as possible.

The Alliance for Climate Protection
(650) 543-7395
Web site: www.climateprotect.org

The Alliance for Climate Protection's purpose is to persuade people of the importance, urgency, and feasibility of adopting and implementing effective and comprehensive solutions for the climate crisis. The group advocates nonpartisan alliances, uses innovative and far-reaching communication techniques, and has created the We campaign (www.wecansolveit.org).

Climate Change Skeptic
Web site: climatechangeskeptic.blogspot.com

Maintained by a civil engineer who lives in Texas, this Web site is a "climate change skeptic repository." It includes a collection of newspaper columns and scientific papers that demonstrate the lack of scientific consensus on man-made climate change.

Climate Skeptic
Web site: www.climate-skeptic.com

Run by Warren Meyer, the author of *A Skeptical Layman's Guide to Anthropogenic Global Warming*, this site attempts to represent fairly the case of global warming skeptics. It includes a number of sources and scientific articles, which the author either supports or disputes.

Co-op America
1612 K Street NW, Suite 600, Washington, DC   20006
(800) 584-7336
Web site: www.coopamerica.org

Co-op America's mission is to create a socially just and environmentally sustainable society. It aims to create that through economic power, and it focuses on economic strategies that can solve social and environmental problems. Co-op America also empowers individuals to take both personal and collective action and works to stop "abusive practices."

The Daily Green
Deborah Jones Barrow, Founder, New York, NY   10019
Web site: www.thedailygreen.com

Published by the Digital Media unit of Hearst Magazines, the Daily Green considers itself a "consumers guide to the green revolution." The Web site posts news articles on environmental and climate change issues, information on environmentally conscious homes and food, as well as eco-oriented quizzes, tips, and carbon calculators.

EarthShare
7735 Old Georgetown Road, Suite 900, Bethesda, MD   20814
(800) 875-3863
Web site: www.earthshare.org

EarthShare's mission is to engage individuals and organizations in creating a healthy environment. Among other activities, Earth Share supports a network of America's nonprofit conservation and environmental organizations and works to promote awareness and charitable giving through workplace giving campaigns. The organization also provides news and tips on environmental stewardship.

Environmental Defense Fund (EDF)
257 Park Avenue South, New York, NY   10010
(212) 505-2100 • fax: (212) 505-2375

Web site: edf.org

EDF links science, economics, and law to create innovative, equitable, and cost-effective solutions to society's most urgent environmental problems. The Web site includes detailed information on the organization's work on global warming, endangered species, ocean-related issues, and other climate change and scientific concerns. The site also has information on action that individuals can take.

Green Living Ideas
P.O. Box 2466, Santa Rosa, CA   95450
(877) 548-4733
Web site: greenlivingideas.com

Green Living Ideas provides tips, information, and ideas to help individuals "green" every area of their lives. Authors and experts weigh in with their suggestions on how to lead an environmentally friendly lifestyle, covering such topics as fashion and beauty, home care, and travel.

Heartland Institue
19 South LaSalle Street, Suite 903, Chicago, IL   60603
(312) 377-4000
e-mail: think@heartland.org
Web site: www.heartland.org

The Heartland Institute's mission is to discover, develop, and promote free-market solutions to social and economic problems. The institute promotes common-sense environmentalism and presents its ideas on how to best maintain a healthy environment. The site also has an archive of public-policy documents and links to their various publications.

Ideal Bite
Web site: www.idealbite.com

Ideal Bite's mission is to create a more sustainable world by connecting enlightened companies with responsible consumers who are interested in taking personal action to combat climate change. One feature of the site is "Daily Tips," which covers a range of topics, including organic cosmetics and eco-friendly pet products.

Intergovernmental Panel on Climate Change (IPCC)

41-22-730-8208/84
e-mail: IPCC-Sec@wmo.int
Web site: www.ipcc.ch

The IPCC was set up by the World Meteorological Organization and the United Nations Environment Programme to provide decision makers and others interested in climate change with an objective source of information about the topic. The site includes IPCC reports, press information, graphics, and speeches.

TreeHugger

850 3rd Avenue, 8th Floor, New York, NY   10022
Web site: www.treehugger.com

TreeHugger is dedicated to driving sustainability mainstream. Its Web site has a great deal of information about green news, solutions, and product information conveyed through blogs, daily and weekly newsletters, a radio show, and video segments.

U.S. Environmental Protection Agency (EPA)
Climate Change Division

Ariel Rios Building, 1200 Pennsylvania Avenue, NW
Washington, DC   20460
(202) 343-9990
e-mail: climatechange@epa.gov
Web site: www.epa.gov/climatechange

The Web site of the EPA's Climate Change Division offers comprehensive information on the issue of climate change in a way that is accessible and meaningful to all parts of society—communities, individuals, business, states and localities, and governments. The site offers a range of information on policies, science, health and environmental effects, and action individuals can take.

Worldchanging
1517 12th Avenue, Seattle, WA   98122
Web site: www.worldchanging.com

Worldchanging is an online magazine that believes that the tools, models and ideas for building a better future lie all around us. The magazine discusses innovative and important tools, ideas, and models for building a "green future." In particular, the magazine examines the stories that it feels the mainstream media overlook.

Bibliography

Books

Joseph F.C. DiMento and Patricia Doughman, eds.   *Climate Change: What It Means for Us, Our Children, and Our Grandchildren.* Cambridge, MA: MIT Press, 2007.

Kerry Emanuel with an afterword by Judith A. Layzer and William R. Moomaw   *What We Know About Climate Change.* Cambridge, MA: MIT Press, 2007.

Doug Fine   *Farewell, My Subaru: An Epic Adventure in Local Living.* New York: Villard, 2008.

Al Gore   *An Inconvenient Truth: The Crisis of Global Warming.* New York: Viking Juvenile, 2007.

Grist Press   *Wake Up and Smell the Planet: The Non-Pompous, Non-Preachy Grist Guide to Greening Your Day.* Seattle, WA: Mountaineers Books, 2007.

Christopher C. Horner   *The Politically Incorrect Guide to Global Warming (and Environmentalism).* Washington, DC: Regnery, 2007.

William H. Kemp	*The Renewable Energy Handbook: A Guide to Rural Energy Independence, Off-Grid and Sustainable Living.* Ontario, Canada: Aztext Press, 2006.
Bjørn Lomborg	*Cool It: The Skeptical Environmentalist's Guide to Global Warming.* Knopf, 2007.
William McDonough and Michael Braungart	*Cradle to Cradle: Remaking the Way We Make Things.* New York: North Point Press, 2002.
Elizabeth Rogers	*The Green Book: The Everyday Guide to Saving the Planet One Simple Step at a Time.* New York: Three Rivers Press, 2007.
Matthias Ruth, ed.	*Smart Growth and Climate Change: Regional Development, Infrastructure and Adaptation.* Cheltenham, United Kingdom and Northampton, MA: Elgar, 2006.
Roy Spencer	*Climate Confusion: How Global Warming Hysteria Leads to Bad Science, Pandering Politicians and Misguided Policies That Hurt the Poor.* New York: Encounter Books, 2008.
Richard M. Stapleton, ed.	*Pollution A to Z.* New York: Macmillan Reference Books, 2003.

Periodicals

John A. Bewick — "Energy Technology: Cultivating Clean Tech," *Public Utilities Fortnightly*, May 2008.

Dennis Coday and Rich Heffern — "Midwest Floods: Scientists Link Extreme Weather Patterns with Global Warming," *National Catholic Reporter*, July 11, 2008.

The Economist — "A Changing Climate of Opinion?" September 4, 2008.

Bruce Geiselman — "Faith, Green Groups Find Common Ground," *Waste News*, July 7, 2008.

Meg Green — "Climate Change Increases Claims Exposure," *Best's Review*, July 2007.

Deborah Harford — "A New World," *Canadian Business*, October 8, 2007.

William F. Jasper — "2008 Climate Debate," *The New American*, March 31, 2008.

Steven Mufson — "Climate Change Debate Hinges on Economics," *Washington Post*, July 15, 2007.

Fred Pearce — "Climate Change: Menace or Myth?" *New Scientist*, no. 2486, February 12, 2005.

Elisabeth Rosenthal — "Changing Climate Haunting Tourism," *International Herald Tribune*, October 30, 2007.

R. Shaw, M. Colley, and R. Connell   "Climate Change Adaptation by Design: A Guide for Sustainable Communities," *Town and County Planning Association*, 2007.

Barrett Sheridan and George Wehrfritz   "The New Green Leaders," *Newsweek International*, May 5, 2008.

Space Daily   "Record Land Grab Feared in Poor Forested Countries," July 14, 2008.

Peter N. Spotts   "Time to Begin 'Adapting' to Climate Change?" *Christian Science Monitor*, February 13, 2007.

Matt Tyrnauer   "Industrial Revolution, Take Two," *Vanity Fair*, May 2008.

Bryan Walsh   "Why Green Is the New Red, White and Blue," *Time*, April 28, 2008.

Index